COINS
AND COIN COLLECTING

COINS
AND COIN COLLECTING

by Seymour Reit   illustrated by W. T. Mars

GOLDEN PRESS NEW YORK

U.S. $1 gold piece (large size)

ACKNOWLEDGMENTS

The author and editors wish to express their appreciation to all those who gave their time and help, and particularly to the following individuals and organizations: Mr. Henry Grunthal, Curator, the American Numismatic Society; Mr. James Ginty, the Dag Hammarskjöld Foundation; the Whitman Publishing Company; Mr. Herbert Aaron; and the Chase Manhattan Bank Public Relations Department for their help in providing so many of the photographs in this book.

PICTURE CREDITS

German thaler (1778).
These were paid to Hessians
for fighting American Colonists

Italian ten-lire piece (obverse)

TABLE OF CONTENTS

*Japanese money tree (1835).
Coins were broken off as needed*

Early U.S. mint issue disme (1792)

*1918 "S" quarter
with overstrike on date (reverse)*

COLLECTING COINS

U.S. $5 gold piece (1915)

Japanese ten-sen piece (1938)

French fifty-franc piece

U.S. $10 gold piece

Coin collecting is one of the most popular of all hobbies. Like people who dig for buried treasure, collectors can always hope to find items of great value. And because even a coin that is worth very little today may be worth many times as much in twenty years, collecting coins often becomes a lifetime hobby. But the *real* fun is in watching your collection grow and improve, little by little, day by day.

How does a coin collector get started? The answer is simple. Each of us, whether we realize it or not, is a collector right now. Right in our pockets, or our purses, are coins which can form the base of a good collection. We can simply begin with the coins we have, and build from there.

Of course, we must decide *what* we wish to collect. Shall it be American coins? Canadian? Shall we collect animal coins? Portraits? Coins showing ships or buildings? Should we specialize in commemoratives? How about a "little of everything?" There are no rules to follow. Everyone is free to collect whatever gives him the most satisfaction and enjoyment.

Once a decision is made, the next problem is *where* to look for the items we need. Let's suppose we've decided to collect American coins. Many of these come into our hands every day. We can enlist our friends and relatives in the hunt, telling them which coins are needed. Neighborhood storekeepers can sometimes be drafted into the search. Some of the scarcer pieces may not be easy to locate. If necessary, these can be bought from dealers, or from members of a local coin club. But the experience of most collectors shows that 95 percent of their collections came from coins passing through their hands in normal day-to-day activities.

Here are a few tips to help you in building a collection:
- Empty your pockets every night. Go through your coins carefully, checking dates, mint marks, and so on.
- Try to get as many coins as possible in change. If, for example, you're saving Lincoln cents, don't give a store-

keeper a penny for one piece of gum. Pay him with a nickel. You'll get four cents in change, which means four more chances to find the coin you're after.

- Make a checklist of the gaps in your collection. Carry it with you at all times. After a while, you'll be able to keep missing dates and mint marks in your memory.

- Buy a coin catalogue which has the latest dealer prices on all coins. Circle the items you need. Save up for them. Perhaps your family or friends can give you coins as gifts, for birthdays or other occasions.

- Join a coin club in your city or neighborhood. Exchange ideas and information with other collectors. Learn all you can about your fascinating hobby.

Naturally, the more you know about coins the more you will enjoy collecting them. So let's begin with the story behind your hobby: what money is, why it was needed, and how it first came into being.

Athenian tetradrachm (478-336 B.C.)

Russian three-kopeck piece

Booker T. Washington U.S. commemorative half dollar

Privately issued U.S. copper token showing Martha Washington on the obverse and the words "Don't tread on me" on the reverse

Reverse of African one-dollar piece issued by the Sierra Leone Company

German "bell" thaler (1643)

Alaskan token

9

HOW MONEY STARTED

Chimgawa walked slowly through the forest. On his back he carried the carcass of a young deer. The hunt had been successful, and there would be meat for his hungry family. But Chimgawa was troubled. During the chase he had lost a valuable spearhead. Spearheads had to be chipped slowly from very hard rock, and they took a long time to make.

Near the Indian village, Chimgawa saw Nekondeg sitting in front of his wickiup, warming himself in the sun. Nekondeg made the finest spear and arrowheads of anyone in the tribe, but he was getting old, and he couldn't run and hunt as well as the younger braves. The two men spoke together. Nekondeg gave Chimgawa a fine new spearhead; in return, Chimgawa gave him part of his deer.

Years ago, this type of trading, called *barter*, was very common. Before the creation of money, barter was the best way for people to get the goods and products they needed. Trading was carried on not only by individuals but by whole tribes and villages. One village, for instance, might have rich soil for raising grain. A nearby tribe might have skilled weavers who made beautiful cloth for shirts and blankets. So the two groups would come together to exchange their goods. This was done for many years, and is still being done in primitive parts of

Africa and Australia. But as civilization developed, and life grew more complex, a better method was needed. Barter goods were too heavy to carry for long distances. It wasn't always possible to have the right things at the right time. And people didn't always want what their neighbors made. So the idea of money came into being.

At first, money was anything which *stood for* a certain amount of goods. Today, for example, we say our money has "purchasing power." It represents a certain amount of food, clothing, books, or anything else we care to buy. If we want food, we no longer carry barter goods to the store. Instead, we pay for our food with money. The storekeeper then uses this money to buy the things which *he* wants.

Early money took many forms. The descendants of Chimgawa and Nekondeg used beads and shells. But almost anything could serve, as long as it followed a few simple rules:

1) It had to be accepted as money by others in the community
2) It had to have some value itself
3) In most cases, it had to be easy to carry
4) It had to be made of strong material, so that it could be passed along from one person to another without wearing out too quickly

The step from barter to money took place centuries ago. In today's complex world it may no longer seem important, but it helped start man on the long march toward civilization.

FISHHOOKS, SALT, AND TIGER CLAWS

*Tooth money
(South Sea Islands)*

Ax money (Mexico)

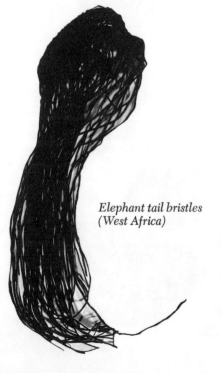

*Elephant tail bristles
(West Africa)*

In the South Pacific, there is an island called Yap. Scattered about this island are many huge, wheel-like stones. Each has a hole in the center. When a pole is put through, the heavier ones can be carried by several men. Centuries ago, the people of Yap used these stones as money. They were carved from limestone found on the Palaus Islands, or Guam, many hundreds of miles away. Then the great stone wheels were floated to Yap on ocean-going rafts. The Yap islanders believed that the larger the stone, the more it was worth. Although many are small, some are as much as ten feet across!

One ambitious islander tried to carve a stone eighteen feet wide, but it cracked before he finished it. Today, these stones are sometimes used in village ceremonies. But civilization has caught up with tiny Yap. Her strange "coins" have no value now except as historic relics.

Yap money was unusual because of its size. Most primitive money was small enough to be carried comfortably. Money could be almost anything chosen by the particular tribe or community. In some cases, the choice had magic or religious meaning. But in many cases, the item was practical and useful.

In Alaska, bunches of fishhooks tied together were used as money. The natives of Mexico used soap. Mongolian money consisted of pieces of silk. In China, "tea money" was common. This was made of tea leaves and sawdust, pressed into the shape of a small brick. The teeth of wild dogs, strung together on a necklace, were used in the Solomon Islands. Whale teeth served as money in the Fiji Islands. In Portuguese West Africa, a man was considered rich if he owned some elephant tail bristles. Other tribes used human hair and tiger claws.

In the lands around the Baltic Sea, amber was of great value. This yellowish-brown substance served not only as money but as a magic charm. Many people believed it could cure ills and bring good luck. One item of great value in parts of Africa was salt. It was packed in special containers of bamboo, several feet long. Roman soldiers were often paid in salt. Our word "salary" comes from the Latin word *salarium,* which means "salt rations." To this day, we speak of a lazy worker as someone who is "not worth his salt."

The North American Indians used a currency called *wampum.* This consisted of beads made from seashells, threaded together in a strip, or belt. There were two main kinds of wampum—white and purple. Sometimes black took the place of purple. Wampum was very important in early times, and was accepted as legal money in the colonies as late as 1661. Besides wampum, American colonists used nails, fur, tobacco, and musket balls.

Another type of shell money is called *cowrie.* The cowrie is a small, yellowish-white, shiny shell. It is one of the oldest of all forms of money, and is still used in parts of Africa and the South Seas.

Many kinds of strange money were made of precious metal. The Aztec people of Mexico paid their debts with small, doll-like figures made of solid gold. In ancient Egypt, "ring money" was popular. These rings came in many shapes and sizes, and were made of bronze, copper, or gold. In those days, people liked to wear all their wealth on their arms, legs, and fingers. Ring money was also used by the Celts of ancient Ireland. In China, flat pieces of bronze were used. Because of their shape, they were known as "knife money" and "spade money." In the Belgian Congo, the natives invented a very special kind of money. It consisted of a piece of copper in the rough shape of an "X," and it was used for the sole purpose of buying a wife!

In many parts of the world, cattle and oxen were used as money, as well as such foods as rice, bread, and chocolate. But this kind of money was hard to store and carry, and it often went bad. On the other hand, metal such as gold or bronze *never* went bad. So people everywhere began to rely more and more on precious metal as the best and most sensible "medium of exchange." This paved the way for man's next big step forward—the invention of coins.

Aztec gold (Mexico)

Tea money (Siberia)

Ring money (Ivory Coast)

13

THE FIRST COINS

*Lydian stater
(made of electrum)*

The honor of creating the very first coins goes, say most historians, to the kingdom of Lydia. This ancient land was located in Asia Minor, on the Aegean Sea. Its capital was a great city called Sardis. Under King Gyges, it became the most powerful state of its time.

Lydian coins were first struck about 2,700 years ago. They were small, oval-shaped bits of metal made of *electrum*, a

mixture of gold and silver. The coins were stamped with various symbols, and were issued in different sizes.

Precious metals had been used before, but not in coin form. The metal—gold, silver, copper, and so on—was carried in the form of bars or chunks. Before each sale, these had to be weighed by money dealers in the market place to decide their value. Later on, the rough, uneven bars and chunks were stamped with a *die* to mark their weight. The dies were wedge-shaped pieces of very hard metal called "coins." When Lydia created its standard, oval-shaped bits of money, the word

Aeginean stater (earliest silver coin)

One of the first coins of pure gold, created by King Croesus. It showed the heads of a lion and a bull facing each other. These beasts were ancient symbols of power

"coin" was used to describe them, and has been used ever since.

In Lydia and its neighboring lands, the little oval coins became very popular. At last people could trade in the market place without confusion. They knew exactly what their metal was worth because the amount was stamped right on it. It was also much easier for people to make change. And, since the coins were issued by the government itself, everyone was willing to take them in payment.

The last king of Lydia, a ruler named Croesus, is believed to have created the first coins of pure gold. King Croesus was known for his great wealth. Nowadays, people still use the phrase "as rich as Croesus."

The citizens of Lydia were great travelers and traders. On their journeys they carried many of their cleverly stamped coins, using them to buy goods and services. Other areas began adopting this convenient type of money, and the use of coins slowly spread. Lydian coins are still in existence, but centuries ago the kingdom became a part of the Persian Empire.

All that remains today of once great Lydia are a few handfuls of ancient coins, her small but priceless gift to the world.

Early coins were oval bits of metal, stamped with a die to mark their weight

COINS OF GREECE AND ROME

Like links in an invisible chain, the coins of Greece and Rome are our links with the distant past. Ancient Greece was made up of great cities and city-states, such as Aegina, Corinth, Syracuse, Athens, and Sparta. Each of these centers had its own coinage, and they competed to create coins of great beauty and richness.

In those days, coins were not only a means of exchange. They were also treated as religious charms, or "talismans," with magic power. Most early coins had pictures of Greek gods and goddesses on them, and symbolic creatures of all kinds, from turtles to winged horses.

Coin of ancient Thrace showing Alexander and the goddess Athena holding "Victory"

Greek coinage began in the seventh century B.C., about 2,500 years ago. The Lydians invented coins, but the Greeks improved on these, giving them a more standard shape and metal content. They also created coins of different values. The chief metal used was silver. As the Greek city-states grew in power and wealth, their coins became tiny perfections of the sculptor's art. To this day, they are judged to be the most beautiful coins of all time.

Many coins were miniature copies of actual sculpture. The head of the sun god Helios, on the coins of Rhodes, was probably based on the famed Colossus of Rhodes, one of the Seven Wonders of the Ancient World. The statue of Pallas Athena in the Parthenon, carved by the sculptor Phidias, was used on the Athenian coins called *tetradrachms*. The famous statue "Victory of Samothrace," now in the Louvre in Paris, appears in miniature on the coins of Macedonia.

Coin of Sidon, chief city of ancient Phoenicia, showing a ship and a chariot

The basic coin of Greece was the silver *drachma*. Silver was not used just for its beauty or value, but for another reason as well. In those days, citizens of Athens carried small coins in their mouths, so it was necessary to use a metal that tasted pleasant! Other popular coins were the tetradrachm, worth four drachmas, and the *dekadrachm*, worth ten drachmas. The dekadrachm was a large silver piece, used as a medallion as

Tetradrachm of Athens showing the goddess Athena and her owl, a symbol of wisdom

17

Silver dekadrachm of Syracuse, generally considered one of the world's most beautiful coins. It was struck about 412 B.C. to commemorate the Syracusan victory over the invading Athenian armies

well as a coin. It was issued to mark special events, festivals, and military victories. Most beautiful of all were the deka-drachms of the city of Syracuse.

The basic coin of the Romans was the *denarius*. A denarius was worth half a Greek drachma. The standard gold coin was the *aureus*. It was valued at twenty-five denarii, and was introduced by Julius Caesar. Roman coins, while not as perfect as those of Greece, are still fine examples of coin making. They also give us much information about Roman life in those times.

The oldest Roman coin was the *as*. It was made of bronze, and was very large, but it was re-issued later in smaller and smaller sizes. The *as* was used about the way our copper pennies are used today. The first of these coins showed the head of the god Janus on one side, and the prow of a ship on the other. The boys of ancient Rome tossed coins just as boys do today. But instead of crying, "Heads or tails!" they cried, "Capita aut navem!" which means, "Heads or ship!" In coin

language, the "head" side is now called the *obverse*. The "tail" side is called the *reverse*.

Like the Greeks, the Romans used pictures of gods on their coins, as well as mythical and religious symbols. The Romans were very proud of their great buildings, and these began appearing on their coins. The bronze *sesterce* of the emperor Titus showed the famed Colosseum, where gladiators fought to the death. The sesterces of the emperor Trajan showed the Circus Maximus, another great arena. The Circus Maximus could seat 260,000 people—about three times as many as can fit into Yankee Stadium.

Another coin of Trajan's, a bronze *as,* carries a picture of a bridge which the emperor built over the Danube River. Some coins show the temple of Juno Moneta, where the Roman mint was located. Juno Moneta was the deity who guarded coins. From her name come our own words "money" and "mint."

Later on, Roman coins began to carry portraits of historic

Bronze sesterce of Trajan showing the Circus Maximus, a Roman arena where great gladiatorial contests and chariot races were held

*Roman denarius showing
the emperor Augustus Caesar*

*Dilepton of Pontius Pilate,
issued in Judea*

*Double Victoriatus issued in
Thessaly, on the Aegean Sea*

figures on the obverse (head) side. Among them were Julius Caesar, Marc Antony, Cleopatra, and Brutus. All of Rome's emperors and empresses were shown on coins, including Augustus, Tiberius, Caligula, Hadrian, and the infamous Nero. In many cases, these wonderful coins are our only clue as to what these historic people really looked like. Roman coinage also showed miniatures of roadways, aqueducts, religious buildings, and triumphal arches.

Though Greek coins were more beautiful, Rome's coins have had a greater effect on modern design. Symbols such as wreaths, stars, and eagles were first used by the Romans. The Liberty cap, worn by our goddess of Liberty, was actually a cap worn by Roman slaves who had been given their freedom. The *fasces*, a bundle of rods wrapped around an ax, was a Roman symbol of authority. This appeared on the reverse (tail) side of the American dime from 1916 to 1945. The mint mark, stamped on a coin to show where it was made, was invented by Roman coin makers. They also began the custom of printing words in a curve, to fit around the coin's edge.

Surprisingly, the ancient coins of Greece and Rome are *not* very rare. Good specimens can be bought from dealers for as little as fifty cents each. The reason for this is that great numbers of these coins were made. Since metal is a tough substance, they have survived over many centuries. In those days there were no banks, and people stored their money everywhere. Piles of coins were hidden at home. Many were buried in the earth, in stone jars called *amphorae*. Coins were also placed in coffins, to be used by the souls of the dead. These hidden and buried coins are still turning up. Scientists, digging in ancient ruins, have collected many of them. Others have been uncovered by farmers, pushing their plows through the rich, history-drenched soil of Greece and Italy.

A collector holding an ancient sesterce and running his fingers over a design of the Colosseum holds a moment of history in his hands. With a little imagination, he might almost hear the shouts of the Roman crowd, the thunder of chariot wheels, and the trumpets of the guard announcing the arrival of the emperor.

EARLY COINS OF OTHER LANDS

After the fall of Greece and Rome, the art of coin making was all but forgotten. Europe was swept by plagues, wars, and famine. Trade between cities of that region dwindled away, and coins in quantity were no longer needed. But in other parts of the world, countries began creating coinage of their own.

In the Norse countries such as Iceland, Scandinavia, and Saxony, fish and cloth money, called *vadmal,* were first used. Next came ring money, then imitations of Roman coins. These were called *stats* and *oras.* Later on, the Norsemen modeled their coins on those of the British Empire. The citizens of Malacca, on the Malay Peninsula, had an unusual type of money made of tin. It was shaped like a tree, and the coins were the branches. When a Malaccan wanted to buy something, he simply broke off a branch of his "money tree."

In China, coins were made chiefly of bronze. They had holes in the middle so they could be strung together on a piece of cord. These coins were known as "cash." This has no connection with our own word "cash," which comes from the French word *caisse,* meaning a box or treasure chest. The Chinese people thought of coins as good luck charms. A coin was often placed in the mouth of a person who died, to serve as a lucky omen.

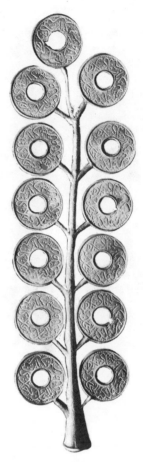

East Indian money tree. Coins were broken off as needed

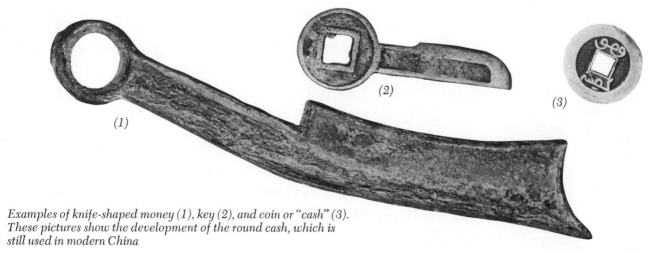

(1)   *(2)*   *(3)*

Examples of knife-shaped money (1), key (2), and coin or "cash" (3). These pictures show the development of the round cash, which is still used in modern China

Renaissance popes did much to encourage the creation of beautiful coinage

Gros tournois
of Philip IV of France

English groat of Henry VIII

During the thirteenth century, in Italy, the art of fine coin making began again. Great sculptors like Benvenuto Cellini and Leonardo da Vinci designed coins for kings, popes, and ruling families. One of the best-known coins of this time was the Venetian *ducat*. Many beautiful coins were made during the Renaissance period by the Vatican. A good example is the gold coin with a portrait of Pope Clement VIII, issued in 1592. During this same era, France's King Louis IX started a system of French coinage. One type of gold piece, called a *gros tournois,* became the standard coin throughout Europe. In England, the same type of coin was called a *groat.*

Our word "dollar" comes from a German coin called a *thaler,* a large silver piece first struck in 1518. Silver for these coins came from the mines of Joachimsthal, in Bohemia.

"Gun money"
of James II of Ireland

These *Joachimsthalers*, or thalers, carrying a figure of St. Joachim on the obverse, were highly popular in Europe for four hundred years. In 1871, the basic German money unit was changed from the thaler to the *mark*.

Russian coinage didn't get under way until the Tartar invaders were driven from the country in the fifteenth century. Russia's basic coin, the *ruble*, first appeared in 1547. For a while, under the empress Catherine I, rubles were issued in square shapes.

An interesting coin of the Middle Ages is the Hungarian hundred-ducat gold piece. It carries a portrait of Ferdinand III, who ruled the Holy Roman Empire in the seventeenth century. This coin, one of the largest ever minted, was three inches across and weighed over two pounds!

Joachimsthaler
of Bohemia (obverse)

Gold coin of Darius,
king of Persia

Modern "gun money"—an emergency
note issued during the Boer War

Isle of Man half penny
(three-legged design)

Guadelupe Holey dollar
and "dump"

The earliest dated coin,
an Austrian tyrol (1484)

In 1689 and 1690, in Ireland, King James II issued "gun money." It was called this because the coins were made from scrap metal such as old cannons, bells, and even kitchen pots. King James, who had been driven from the English throne, planned to pay the holders of his makeshift coins when he won back his royal status. But this never happened, and Irish gun money became almost worthless. Money of this kind, created for a special need or emergency, is known as "money of necessity." It is also called "siege money," because it was often used by a besieged city in wartime. Siege money has been made out of all types of materials—not only precious metal, but china, leather, wood, stamps, and even cut-up playing cards.

An unusual design of earlier years was the "triskelion." This was used on ancient Sicilian coins, and on the copper coins of the Isle of Man issued in the eighteenth century. The "triskelion" design consists of three huge running legs, joined together at the hip. The Latin motto on the Isle of Man coinage means: "Wherever you toss it, it will stand."

Another unusual coin was the "Holey dollar" of Australia. In the early days, Australians used Spanish silver dollars, but a smaller, less expensive coin was needed. So, in 1813, the center of the Spanish dollar was punched out. This formed two separate coins. One was a large coin with a hole in the center —the Holey dollar—and the other was a small round token. The smaller coin, marked "fifteen pence," was called a *dump*.

One of the most famous of all money units is the English *pound*. In ancient Rome, the *libra* was the standard weight unit, equaling a pound of silver. The English pound also started as a measure of weight. It stood for the exact amount of metal needed to make 240 silver pennies. Today's pound, issued in paper form, is used in England, Australia, Israel, and Egypt. Another well-known English coin is the *shilling*. It was made of silver, and was first issued during the reign of King Henry VII. For many years in England and her colonies, the phrase "to take the King's shilling" meant to enlist in the army. Henry VII's profile, appearing on this coin, was created by Alexander de Brugsal. It is one of the finest examples of coin sculpture in the world.

PORTRAITS ON COINS

The first man to have his image on a coin was Alexander the Great. Before then, only portraits of gods and goddesses were used. But after Alexander died, in 323 B.C., a former general of his named Lysimachus wanted to honor him in a special way. Lysimachus was then the king of Thrace. So he ordered a new tetradrachm issued, with Alexander's profile on the obverse.

Later on, the Ptolemies, kings of Egypt, began to put their own portraits on their coinage. From the time of Julius Caesar, Rome's emperors also placed their faces on coins. The reverse side often showed a military victory, a public building, or some other scene glorifying the reign. These coins were a kind of "advertising" method, showing people what their ruler looked like, and helping to make him popular.

Mozart (Austria)

William Tell (Switzerland)

In the Middle Ages, many kings, queens, and popes were pictured on coins. Saints were also shown, as well as national heroes. Sometimes the monarch was pictured as an infant. One example of this is a Spanish five-*peseta* piece, showing King Alfonso XIII as a baby. Coins of the Vatican carried beautiful portraits. Outstanding were the *scudos* of Pope Clement VIII and Pope Innocent XI.

Copernicus (Poland)

25

Ptolemy I (Egypt)

Cleopatra (Egypt)

Augustus (Rome)

Caesar (Rome)

King Perseus (Macedon)

King Philip V (Macedon)

King George III (Great Britain)

Francis Joseph I (Austria-Hungary)

In one case, a king's portrait turned into a national joke. During the reign of Henry VIII of England, a shilling was struck showing a full-face view of the famous ruler. The coins, issued in 1544, were supposed to be silver, but were really made of copper with a thin coating of silver on top. Little by little the silver began to rub off, leaving the king's nose a bright, shiny copper! Because of this, Henry VIII was sometimes called "Old Coppernose."

France's coinage during the French Revolution and the Napoleonic era carried fine portraits. One silver five-*franc* piece showed a profile of Napoleon wearing a wreath of laurel leaves. Napoleon had always dreamed of ruling a huge empire, and the laurel wreath was a symbol of power first used by the emperors of ancient Rome.

An interesting portrait coin was issued by Saxony in 1610. This silver thaler carried a picture of not one but *four* Saxon dukes. Another outstanding thaler is the Maria Theresa thaler of Austria. Although issued for 150 years, this coin always carried the date 1780.

During the 1920's and 1930's, the republics of Germany and Austria turned out many beautiful portrait coins. One series was issued by the Austrian government to honor its great musicians. Shown on these coins are Franz Schubert, Wolfgang

Mozart, Joseph Haydn, and Ludwig van Beethoven. A good example of the hero portrait is the five-franc silver piece of Switzerland, with a bust of William Tell. According to legend, Tell led an uprising of Swiss patriots against the rule of Austria in 1308. As a punishment, he was forced to shoot an apple off his son's head, but the legend says that he performed this feat successfully.

Alfonso XIII (Spain)

Simón Bolívar, known as the liberator of South America, appears on coins of many South American countries, among them Colombia and Venezuela. The Venezuelan coin is actually called a *bolívar*.

Simón Bolívar (Venezuela)

Today, many rulers and national figures are pictured on coins. England, for example, shows Queen Elizabeth II, Holland shows Queen Juliana, and Sweden shows King Gustav VI. Since 1858, Canadian coins have carried the faces of English monarchs. American coins have shown portraits of Washington, Jefferson, Franklin, Lincoln, F. D. Roosevelt, and Kennedy. Those portraits are all in profile—only one side of the face appears.

Balboa (Panama)

United States commemorative coins, issued for special occasions, have also carried portraits. Among the famous Americans shown are Robert E. Lee, Daniel Boone, and Stephen Foster.

Fuad I (Egypt)

Franz Schubert (Austria)

Pope John XXIII (Vatican City)

Sun Yat Sen (China)

Santos Dumont (Brazil)

GODS, DRAGONS, AND WINGED HORSES

Centuries ago, according to legend, Greece was troubled by a fierce monster called a "Chimera." It was part goat, part lion, and part dragon, and it caused great havoc in the land. One day a young warrior named Bellerophon came to court. Because of a family feud, Greece's King Iobates wanted to get rid of Bellerophon, so he sent him to fight the Chimera.

Pallas Athena, the Greek goddess of wisdom, felt sorry for Bellerophon. She owned a wonderful horse named Pegasus, which could fly through the air as straight and swift as an arrow from Diana's magic bow. She gave this horse to Bellerophon. Riding Pegasus, the warrior fought the Chimera and killed it.

Coin of ancient Corinth showing Pegasus and Pallas Athena

King Iobates then gave the youth other dangerous tasks, but riding his winged horse, Bellerophon accomplished them all. The king finally realized that Bellerophon was favored by the gods. So he gave him his daughter's hand, and named him successor to the throne.

Unfortunately, all this success went to Bellerophon's head. He grew proud and arrogant. One day, he mounted Pegasus and started to fly up to heaven itself. Zeus, father of the gods, grew angry at this. He sent a bee to sting Pegasus. The horse reared, and Bellerophon fell to his destruction.

Today, Pegasus lives on not just in stories and legends but in silver, etched into the coinage of long ago. The winged horse appears most often on coins of the Greek city of Corinth. This was a great seaport. Corinthian ships, manned by brave crews, traveled far and wide. Perhaps this led them to choose as their symbol a winged horse, the greatest of all voyagers.

Coin of Great Britain showing King George III and St. George slaying the dragon

Roman coin showing the god Janus looking both ways

Roman coin showing Hercules on one side and Romulus and Remus, the legendary founders of Rome, on the other

Roman coin showing Mars, god of war, and symbols of empire

Roman coin showing the goddess of health

Many other Greek cities used symbols and make-believe figures on their coinage. The coins of Colophon show a lyre, symbolizing Apollo, the god of music and song. The head of Apollo also appears on the gold *staters* issued by Philip II of Macedon, father of Alexander the Great. The tetradrachms of Athens carry a portrait of Pallas Athena, guardian spirit of the city. The reverse of this coin shows the Athenian owl, symbol of wisdom. Silver staters of the island of Aegina show a tortoise, emblem of Aphrodite. Aegina was an important center of trade, and Aphrodite, goddess of the moon and the seas, was looked on as the protector of commerce.

One of the most unusual myths deals with a coin known as "Charon's Fee." Charon was the aged sailor who supposedly ferried the souls of the dead across the River Styx into Hades. In ancient Greece it was the custom to put a small coin, such as an *obolus*, in the mouth of a dead person. This coin could then be used to pay for the soul's passage across the mysterious river. This custom was continued by the Romans and later by the British. In 1766, the body of King Canute was found in England's Winchester Cathedral. In his hand was a silver penny. So the British believed that even a king must pay Charon's Fee!

The Romans, like the Greeks, put gods and heroes on their coinage. The bronze *as* carried a portrait of Janus, the Roman god of beginnings. He was also the keeper of gates and doors, so he was shown having *two* heads, which helped him to look both ways at the same time.

Some coins showed the powerful Hercules carrying a club and a lion skin. It was Hercules who performed the Twelve Tasks set by the king of Argos. These included slaying the nine-headed Hydra and cleaning the Augean stables. Other deities, or gods, pictured on Roman coins include Diana, goddess of the hunt; Saturn, god of the harvest; Venus, goddess of beauty; and Vulcan, god of fire and iron.

One coin shows Romulus, supposedly the founder of Rome. Legend says that Romulus and his twin brother, Remus, were cast adrift in a basket on the Tiber river. The babies were found by a she-wolf who reared them as if they were her own cubs.

When he reached manhood, Romulus learned that the gods had chosen him to start a great new city. After Rome was founded, Romulus supposedly disappeared in a thunderstorm.

Other lands besides Greece and the Roman Empire have used legendary people and make-believe animals to decorate their coins. In the Orient, for example, dragons are looked on as good and kind friends. For many years, Japanese and Chinese coins have shown decorative dragons. In the fairy tales of the Western world dragons are usually portrayed as villains, keeping "fair damsels" imprisoned in stone towers. The English silver *crown*, issued by George III in 1818, carries on its reverse the famous scene of St. George slaying the dragon. The phoenix appears on Japanese coins. This magic bird was supposed to have a charmed life. When it died, it was burned on a funeral fire, but each time it sprang up alive from its own ashes. The unicorn, another mythical beast, appears on the coins of England, Scotland, and Canada. This animal symbolized purity and gentleness.

The figure of Liberty, used on many United States coins, represents our American ideal of freedom. This legendary lady is descended from two Roman goddesses, Libertas and Roma. The United States dime, issued between 1916 and 1945, shows Liberty wearing a winged headdress. It is often called the Mercury dime because the portrait looks like Mercury, the Roman god of speed and commerce.

Imaginary figures appear on coins of other countries, too, among them Sweden and India. But it is the coinage of Greece and Rome that gives us the richest treasures of myth and legend. On these small bits of metal, the gods and beasts of Mount Olympus, home of the gods, seem almost to "live" again. Here, once more, Hercules wields his mighty club, Vulcan hurls his thunderbolt, and beautiful Pegasus soars aloft on wings of shining silver.

Two Roman coins featuring Diana, goddess of the hunt. One shows a deer, the other a hound

Greek coin showing Poseidon, god of the sea, wielding his trident

Roman coin showing Ceres, the goddess of agriculture

Greek coin of Elis showing the goddess Hera, queen of Olympus

31

Canadian five-cent piece

Canadian twenty-five-cent piece

Australian penny

South African five-shilling piece

A ZOO IN MINIATURE

Irish half crown

The only wild animals most people have a chance to see are those in the zoo. But coin collectors can study the fascinating world of animals whenever they wish, without ever leaving their comfortable armchairs.

Many countries have used animals in their coin designs. The animals shown are usually the kind found in that part of the world. Canada, for example, has the head of a caribou on its twenty-five-cent piece. Canadian five-cent pieces show a beaver. Coins of India show a Brahma bull. The kangaroo appears on the Australian *florin*. The five-shilling piece of South Africa shows a beautiful animal called a springbok. The spring-bok is a type of gazelle. It is noted for its graceful movement and the way it can spring suddenly into the air and dart off. The two-shilling piece of Southern Rhodesia shows an antelope. Another African coin, from Somalia, shows the head of an elephant, complete with huge tusks.

California Diamond Jubilee U.S. commemorative half dollar

The lion, a symbol of courage and royal splendor, appears on the coins of many lands. Among them are Belgium, Holland, Canada, Ethiopia, and Iran. Sometimes it is shown alone. On other coins, the lion is part of a design which includes a shield, stars, a wreath, and perhaps another animal. This is known as a "heraldic" emblem. In earlier times, every important family had its own heraldic designs and banners. Knights often carried such emblems on their shields.

Italian five-lire piece

In the United States, a familiar coin animal is the buffalo. It appears on the reverse of our nickel, minted from 1913 to

African one-dollar piece

Ceylon coin

Australian shilling

Irish penny

Burmese rupee

New Zealand florin

Note the similarity between eagles on this U.S. trade dollar and the Roman tetradrachm of the emperor Hadrian

1938. This animal symbolized the great American West of pioneer days.

Among domestic animals, the horse is the most popular. It gallops and prances nobly across many coin faces, including those of Ireland, Romania, Italy, Luxemburg, and England. One of the most beautiful examples is the ancient dekadrachm of the Greek city of Syracuse. On the reverse side are four magnificent stallions pulling a chariot. Ireland, a country of farming people, has a whole barnyard on its coinage. Among the farm animals shown on Irish florins, shillings, and *pence* are a bull, a rabbit, a sow, and even a mother hen with her brood of chicks.

Birds, like animals, have been widely used. The famous staters of Athens showed an owl, symbol of wisdom. Some Australian florins show a peculiar bird called a kiwi. A coin issued by the Vatican shows the dove of peace. English *farthings* carry a wren. Burmese *rupees* display a proud peacock. The francs of Madagascar, off the coast of East Africa, show a rooster.

The most popular and best known of all coin birds is the eagle. This creature, symbol of courage, independence, and freedom, first appeared on the coins of Rome. Today, the eagle appears on many United States coins, and in many different designs. Sometimes the American eagle has its wings folded. On other coins it is in full flight. Some coins show the eagle with outstretched wings, holding a cluster of arrows in one claw and an olive branch in the other. Experts say that the two most beautiful eagle designs on American coins are the copper Flying Eagle cent, issued from 1856 to 1858, and the Double Eagle gold coin issued from 1907 to 1933. This $20 gold piece was designed by the famous sculptor Augustus Saint-Gaudens.

The eagle has also been used on the coinage of Russia, Poland, England, and Austria. But the credit for first showing this magnificent winged creature goes to the coin makers of ancient Rome. If we compare the eagle on a *tetradrachm* of the emperor Hadrian with one on a United States Trade dollar of 1877, we can see the amazing influence Rome has had on the coins of today.

COINS OF THE BIBLE

"And there came a certain poor widow, and she threw in two mites, which make a farthing . . ."

These words from the Book of Mark tell the story of a poor woman who came to the Temple to make an offering. All she had were two tiny coins, but she gave them humbly and willingly. Historians believe that the "mite" was probably a Roman coin called a *lepton*. Today, the phrase "widow's mite" is used to describe any small offering given with real sincerity.

*Roman lepton
(the "widow's mite")*

There are many such references to coins in both the Old and the New Testaments of the Bible. The *shekel,* mentioned often, was at first a unit of measure. Later it became the chief silver coin of the ancient Hebrews. It was probably created during the first revolt of the Maccabees against the tyranny of the Roman emperor Nero in the year 66. This coin carries a symbolic design of a branch with three lilies, known as "Aaron's Rod." The same design appears today on the silver *prutahs* of Israel.

Ancient Judean shekel

Another coin, mentioned in the Book of Matthew, is the *penny.* Today, our United States one-cent piece is also called a penny. In ancient times this coin was the same as the Roman silver denarius, and was the usual day's pay for a field laborer. The "Tribute Penny" was probably a denarius of the emperor Tiberius. At that time, each citizen of Judea had to pay a yearly tax to Rome. The Bible passage "Render unto Caesar that which is Caesar's" was a reference to this tribute coin paid to the Roman rulers.

*Roman denarius
(the "Tribute Penny")*

Perhaps the best known of all Biblical coins are the "thirty pieces of silver" which the disciple Judas was given for betraying Christ. Scholars now believe that these coins were silver tetradrachms from the city of Tyre.

Many of the coins mentioned in the Bible exist today in museums and private collections. Some can still be bought over the dealer's counter. These time-worn coins act as our mental bridge between today's complex, scientific world and the earlier world of Biblical days.

*Tetradrachm of Tyre
(the "thirty pieces of silver")*

BUCCANEER GOLD

In Robert Louis Stevenson's *Treasure Island*, a parrot perched on Long John Silver's shoulder keeps crying, "Pieces of eight! Pieces of eight!" These words were well known in the seventeenth and eighteenth centuries, especially to sailors who cruised the Spanish Main.

"Piece of eight" was the popular name for the Spanish silver dollar, so called because it was worth eight Spanish *reales*. It was also called a *peso,* and was first minted by the Spanish government, in Mexico City, in 1607. The Mexico City mint

was the first to produce coins in the New World. Between 1732 and 1821, it turned out over *one billion pesos!* These coins were very popular in the West Indies and the American colonies. They were so popular in America that they were accepted as legal money until 1857. This is the only case in American history of a foreign coin being so honored.

The "piece of eight" was designed so it could be cut in half, in order to make change. Half a coin was called "four bits." A quarter of a coin was called "two bits." This is still used as a slang term for our twenty-five-cent piece.

During colonial times, merchant ships sailing the Gulf of Mexico and the Caribbean Sea were often attacked by fierce pirates, and thousands of pesos were taken as loot. Another

Half a coin, or "four bits"

Spanish milled dollar, or "piece of eight"

Quarter of a coin, or "two bits"

*Spanish doubloon,
or eight escudos*

favorite coin of the buccaneers was the Spanish *doubloon*. This was a large, heavy gold piece, minted both in Spain and in Spanish America. At that time, Spain held vast territories in the New World. Her ships made many voyages carrying doubloons for use in trading, buying land, paying the wages of troops, and so on. Other Spanish galleons sailed eastward, carrying ingots of pure silver and gold from the mines of Mexico to the royal coffers of Madrid. All these ships were preyed on by pirate bands, and many rich cargoes fell into their hands. The most famed of these buccaneers were Henry Morgan, William Kidd, and Edward Teach, who was also known as "Blackbeard." Morgan, who helped the British against Spain, was finally knighted by King Charles II, and became the governor of Jamaica. But the others met violent deaths. Captain Kidd was hanged in England and Blackbeard was killed in a battle with a United States naval sloop.

The era of piracy was a short but bloody one. To this day, hidden stores of silver pesos and gold doubloons are still being turned up—ancient mementos of a lawless age.

EARLY COINS OF AMERICA

The first American colonists used beaver skins, tobacco, grain, wampum, musket balls, and gunpowder as money. They also used coins which came their way from foreign lands. English pounds, shillings, and pence were popular. So were Dutch ducats, Spanish doubloons, and French *Louis d'ors.*

Sommer Island (Bermuda) "hog money"

In the 1630's, some copper money came from Bermuda, known long ago as Hog Island. The coins had a picture of a hog on one side and a three-masted ship on the other, and they were called "hog money." Today these coppers are very rare and extremely valuable.

The first coins actually made in America were minted in Boston, Massachusetts. They were shillings and pence, and carried pictures of trees on them—either a willow, an oak, or a pine. These coins were minted from 1652 until 1684. According to legend, the Boston mint master, John Hull, became very rich. When his daughter was married, he gave her a wedding gift consisting of her weight in coins. The story says that Miss Hull, a plump young lady, received 10,000 Pine Tree shillings!

Two pence Rosa Americana (issued in England for use in the colonies)

In the 1720's, some coins were issued in England for special use in the colonies. These were known as the Rosa Americana series. Other interesting coins of the time were the New Constellation cent, which had thirteen stars to represent the thirteen colonies, and the Bar cent, which had the letters USA on one side and thirteen bars on the other. Coins and tokens were also issued by colonial governments and private business firms.

During the American Revolution, soldiers were often paid with Continental paper money, issued by the newly formed Congress and printed in Philadelphia. But people distrusted these bits of paper. They preferred using coins made of reliable metal. The Continental paper money quickly lost value, which led to an expression still heard today, "Not worth a Continental."

Bar cent (1787)

One of the rarest of our early coins is the Brasher Doubloon. This was a large gold piece named after its designer, Ephraim

39

Continental currency
($40—January 14, 1779)

Brasher. It was issued by a private mint in 1787. Only a few samples are still in existence, so they are very valuable. Some years ago, a Brasher Doubloon sold for $6,200. Many other colonial coins, however, can still be bought at low prices.

The first coin *officially* issued by the United States of America was the Fugio cent, dated 1787. On the obverse it carried a sundial and the word *Fugio,* which is Latin for "I fly." A motto on this side reads "Mind Your Business." It was a saying of Ben Franklin's, and in those days it meant "Tend to your business with care." On the reverse side is a chain design with thirteen links, representing the thirteen states of the new nation. Inside the links are the words "We Are One." The Fugio cent was issued in silver, pewter, and brass. Pewter, a favorite metal of the colonists, is an alloy of tin and lead. Early American bowls, mugs, and tableware were often made of pewter. Two hundred years ago it was a fairly commonplace metal, but pewter objects today are valued as antiques.

According to legend, Boston mint master John Hull gave his daughter her weight in Pine Tree shillings as a wedding present

Pine Tree shilling

40

George Washington is supposed to have donated silver plate from his home for use in making early colonial coins

For a few years the only coin issued by the United States government was the Fugio cent. But as the young nation prospered and grew, new coins were badly needed. In 1791, Congress ordered a mint to be built in Philadelphia. This was done, and some dimes and half dimes were issued. It is said that George Washington donated some silver platters from his own home to provide the metal for these early coins.

In 1793, the mint began turning out copper cents and half cents. During the following year silver half dimes, half dollars, and dollars were added to the list. In 1795, the first gold pieces were issued. These were five-dollar and ten-dollar gold coins. In 1796, the mint produced our first quarters. It also turned out a two-and-a-half-dollar gold piece. By the end of the eighteenth century, the Goverment had a busy, well-functioning mint, and ten different types of coins in circulation. Young America was growing up.

Fugio cent (1787). This was the first official coin authorized by the United States Congress

TOKENS, STAMPS, AND "SHINPLASTERS"

Examples of "hard times" tokens

From time to time, other types of coins have been used in America besides the ones minted by the Government.

Jackson cents, also called "hard times tokens," are an example of this. They were issued from 1832 to 1844, during the administration of President Andrew Jackson. In those years business conditions were bad and there was a shortage of copper coins. So various "token" coins were struck by private companies. They took the place of regular coins, and also carried political slogans for or against President Jackson's monetary policies.

In 1848, gold was discovered in California, and the great American gold rush was on. Thousands of fortune hunters raced into the area. Banks were quickly set up. Tradesmen arrived and opened their shops, and business was brisk. But there just weren't enough coins to go around. To solve this shortage, private firms made their own gold pieces. Some were very crude. Others were handsome and well designed. But since they were all made of the precious yellow metal, they were accepted just as readily as United States minted coins. Millions of dollars' worth of pioneer gold coins were turned out, in

values between $5 and $50. Some had odd shapes. One company put out eight-sided coins. Other coins were rectangular. These private coins, called "territorial gold," were issued in other regions also, such as Georgia, North Carolina, and the Mormon Territory in Utah. But most were made in California from 1849 to 1855. Among the companies issuing private gold were Moffat and Co., Templeton Reid, Baldwin and Co., Kellogg and Co., the Pacific Co., the Massachusetts and California Co., and the Miners Bank. Some of these pieces have very high value today. A $5 gold piece issued by the Massachusetts and California Co. in 1849 was recently sold for $7,900. A great many souvenir copies of these private coins have been produced. But there is a simple way to tell genuine coins from souvenir imitations: *only genuine coins have the exact amount stamped on them.*

"Territorial gold"—the obverse of a California $50 gold piece

During the Civil War, a number of Civil War tokens were issued. Once again, there was a shortage of regular coins, so private firms minted their own pennies, with advertising slogans on the backs. Like the gun money of King James, this was "money of necessity."

Advertising token

In the same Civil War era, the Government authorized the use of postage stamps as money. This led to the most unusual of all United States coins. To keep the stamps in good condition, they were placed in small, round brass cases with transparent mica windows. The backs of the brass holders carried ads from

Civil War token

U.S. fractional currency—5c

Confederate paper currency—50c

U.S. fractional currency—50c

the issuing company, such as: "Take Ayer's Pills," "New York Life Insurance Company," and "Dougan the Hatter." Postage stamp money was used in the early 1860's, but was soon replaced by a new kind of paper money called "fractional currency."

Fractional currency was issued between 1862 and 1876. Each bill was worth a certain *fraction* of a dollar—anywhere from three to fifty cents. Thus, instead of a silver dime, a citizen would be given a "paper dime" worth the same amount. But fractional currency proved unpopular and the bills were soon nicknamed "shinplasters." In those days, cuts and bruises were treated with a poultice made of brown paper soaked in vinegar. This was called a "shinplaster." To show their contempt for the new paper money, people called them "shinplasters," too.

Fractional currency is still accepted as legal tender. The United States Treasury Department will redeem any fractional currency at its face value. But this unusual paper money is worth more to collectors. A typical five-cent "shinplaster," spurned by the people of the 1870's, can be sold for two or three dollars today.

American commemorative coin issued in 1954 honoring George Washington Carver

AMERICAN COINS TODAY

Columbian Exposition commemorative

America's growth can be seen in her coinage. In 1795, the total value of all United States coins minted was about $450,000. Fifty years later, in 1845, this amount had jumped to well over $100,000,000!

At present, the United States mints at Philadelphia, Pennsylvania, San Francisco, California, and Denver, Colorado, turn out billions of coins every year. At various times, different kinds of coins were issued and then dropped. A copper two-cent piece, for example, was put out in 1864. But it failed to become popular, and was discontinued in 1873.

Special coins celebrating an historic event, or honoring a famous citizen, have been issued from time to time. These are known as "commemorative" coins. Almost all of them are silver half dollars. Commemorative coins are noted for their beauty. The first one was issued in 1892 in honor of the Columbian Exposition held in Chicago. This great World's Fair marked the 400th anniversary of the discovery of America by Christopher Columbus. The 1892 commemorative half dollar shows a portrait of Columbus on the obverse, and a view of his ship, the *Santa Maria,* on the reverse. The most recent commemorative coin was issued in 1954 to honor the great Negro leader George Washington Carver.

Kennedy half dollar (1964)

45

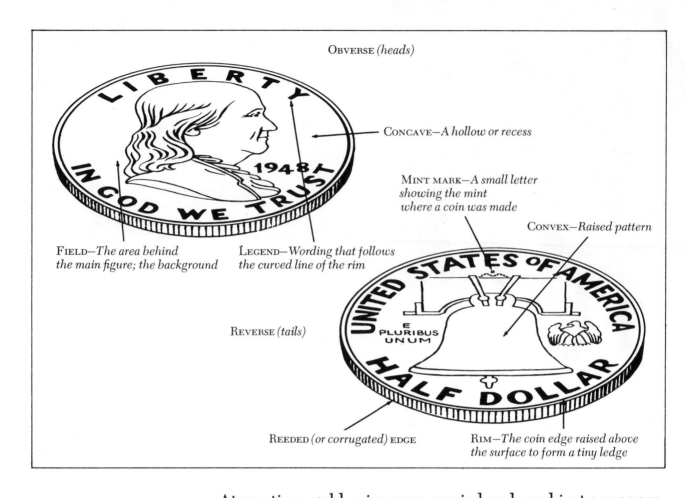

Obverse *(heads)*

Concave—*A hollow or recess*

Mint mark—*A small letter showing the mint where a coin was made*

Convex—*Raised pattern*

Field—*The area behind the main figure; the background*

Legend—*Wording that follows the curved line of the rim*

Reverse *(tails)*

Reeded *(or corrugated)* edge

Rim—*The coin edge raised above the surface to form a tiny ledge*

U.S. Peace dollar, the only coin ever minted to commemorate peace. It was first issued in 1921 as a memorial to the end of World War I

At one time, gold coins were carried and used just as copper, nickel, and silver coins are used now. Gold pieces were minted in values from \$1 to \$20. They were very popular, and were often given as gifts. But in 1933, because of changes in American monetary policy, all gold coins were called in by the Treasury Department. Today, gold pieces can no longer be used in normal buying and selling, but they *can* still be bought and traded for use in coin collections.

Only five types of United States coins are being minted at the present time. These are the:

Lincoln cent . . . . first issued in 1909
Jefferson five-cent piece . . . . first issued in 1938
Roosevelt dime . . . . first issued in 1946
Washington quarter . . . . first issued in 1932
Kennedy half dollar . . . . first issued in 1964

The most recent of our silver dollars was the Peace dollar, minted from 1921 to 1928, and again from 1934 to 1935. It is the only coin issued by any country in this century which carries on it the word "Peace."

MINTS AND MINT MARKS

A workman reaches into a stone furnace with a pair of long-handled tongs. He lifts out a small piece of heated silver and places it on a thick anvil post. Carved on the top of this anvil post is a design for the obverse of a Greek stater. Another man takes a wedge-shaped "punch" and places it on the heated bit of silver. On this punch is a design for the reverse side of the same coin. The man strikes the punch several times with a large hammer, pressing both designs into the silver at the same instant.

Early Roman coin showing Juno Moneta, goddess of money, and some crude coin-making tools

In early coin making, a piece of heated silver was placed on an anvil and struck with a punch. The blow pressed designs into both sides of the soft, heated metal

47

A mint in Renaissance times, showing workmen shaping,
cutting, and stamping coins. Everything was done by hand

Early coins were all made in this way. One by one, the designs on the "dies" were transferred to the precious metal by striking with a hammer. To this day, we say a new coin has been "struck." In ancient Rome, the mint was set up in the temple of Juno Moneta, on Rome's famed Capitoline Hill. Here Roman denarii and sesterces were produced by hand.

Coin making did not change much for many centuries. In the Middle Ages the mints of Europe were only small workrooms in which a handful of craftsmen worked with simple tools. One part of the room was set aside for the delivery and

Early mechanical devices used to roll
metal sheets and stamp out the coins

weighing of raw metal, which is called bullion. This was melted down in brick furnaces into bars, or ingots, and then hammered out into sheets of the right thickness. Round discs were then cut out of these sheets. Next, the discs were struck by dies to produce the finished design.

This method was used until the sixteenth century. At that time the screw press was introduced. By cranking a handle, the screw-press operator forced two dies together, squeezing the coin between them. The machine was first used in Italy, then in France, Germany, and England. Early United States coins were also made on a screw press.

During the late 1500's, a French inventor named Eloye Mestrelle created a machine which rolled metal to the right thickness, cut out blank coins, and stamped a design on them. Mestrelle's coin-making machine could be run either by horse-power or water pressure. The inventor worked for the English during the reign of Queen Elizabeth. Unfortunately, he fell in with a criminal group, and was finally hanged for forgery.

After the invention of steam power, coin machinery underwent a big change. In 1797, James Watts and his partner, Matthew Boulton, began working at the Royal Mint in London, running presses by steam power. The first coin they turned out was a large copper two-penny piece known as a "cartwheel." From then on, hand methods were dropped.

An ancient Greek coining press. Heated metal was held between the tongs, which were then hit with a hammer, pressing the designs into place

An early steam-coining press. Coins were stamped out by steam power, instead of by hand

First coining press used at the Philadelphia mint. This mint was organized in 1793, during George Washington's presidency

49

*Mint at Charlotte, North Carolina
(mint mark "C")*

Philadelphia mint (mint mark "P")

*Mint at Dahlonega, Georgia
(mint mark "D")*

Today's mint is run like any other efficient plant. A modern press turns out in one hour as many coins as several men could produce in one week using old-fashioned screw presses. First, the various metals and alloys are weighed. The balances used are so sensitive that they can pick up differences of 100th of an ounce. After weighing, the metal is melted down in electric furnaces and shaped into bars. These are then rolled into strips of exact thickness. Strips for our cents, for example, must be eight feet long and exactly 48/1000 of an inch thick.

Next, these strips go to punch machines which cut out the coin blanks, called planchets. Five hundred planchets are cut from each strip. The extra metal and trimmings are gathered and re-melted for future use. Now the planchets go to the press room, where high-speed automatic machines stamp the finished coins. These machines operate under very high pressures, depending on the type of coin. In making quarters, eighty tons of pressure is used, while dimes take forty tons. During this stamping process, the edges of the coins are "reeded" with many small up-and-down lines. This makes the edges more durable and protects against counterfeiting. It also prevents dishonest people from shaving or clipping the edges to get extra metal. All United States coins, except cents, have a reeded edge.

Coin presses work at high speeds. A typical press can turn out between 5,000 and 7,500 coins every hour. The finished coins are inspected, weighed, and counted. Finally, they are packed, ready at last to go into circulation.

At one time the dies used in stamping coin designs were made entirely by hand. Today, the process is somewhat different. First a sculptor makes a model that is several times larger than the finished coin will be. A special metal plate is then made from the model. The dies are cut from this by a machine called a pantographic die-cutter. Hundreds of dies are needed at one time to produce America's great quantity of coins. According to law, all dies must be destroyed at the end of each year, and new ones made.

Sculptor creating over-sized model of new coin

Today, the United States operates three mints. The largest mint is at Philadelphia. Branch mints are at Denver and San Francisco. At various times, the United States has operated mints in other parts of the country.

Here is a complete listing of United States mints:

Carson City (Nev.): Organized in 1870 and discontinued in 1893. Mint mark "CC."

Charlotte (N. C.): Organized in 1838 and discontinued in 1861. Gold coins only. Mint mark "C."

Dahlonega (Ga.): Organized in 1838 and discontinued in 1861. Gold coins only. Mint mark "D."

Denver (Colo.): Organized in 1906. Mint mark "D."

New Orleans (La.): Organized in 1837 and discontinued in 1909. Mint mark "O."

Cutting the actual size die with a pantographic die-cutter

Philadelphia (Pa.): Organized in 1793. No mint mark, except for Jefferson nickels issued between 1942 and 1945 that carry the mint mark "P."

San Francisco (Calif.): Organized in 1854, discontinued in 1955, and resumed in 1968. Mint mark "S."

Mint marks are important to collectors because they show the *origin* of a coin. The number of coins produced at some mints has been much smaller than at others. As a result, some issues are very scarce and have become valuable. Except for the Jefferson nickels already mentioned, coins made at the Philadelphia mint do not carry mint marks. Therefore, any coin that turns up without a mint mark can be assumed to have come from the plant at Philadelphia.

Retouching, polishing and cleaning the finished die

(1)

(2)

HOW A MODERN MINT OPERATES

(1) Various metals to be used in coinage are assembled and weighed in exact proportions. Pennies, for example, have 5% zinc and 95% copper. The weighed metal goes to the ingot room in "tote boxes." (2) Furnaces in this room heat the metal until molten. When blended, the metal is poured into molds. (3) The cool ingots are then rolled and pressed into long strips of an exact thickness. (4) Blank coins, called planchets, are then punched from the strips. (5) Next, the planchets go through a stamping machine, where dies stamp designs on both sides. The finished coins are carefully inspected for any possible defects.

(3)

(4)

(5)

(1) Lincoln cent

(2) Jefferson nickel

(7) Mercury dime

(8) Roosevelt dime

(9) Franklin half dollar

(5) Buffalo nickel

(3) Washington quarter

(6) Kennedy half dollar

(4) Morgan dollar

(10) Liberty Standing half dollar

WHERE TO FIND MINT MARKS

(1) LINCOLN CENT: on the obverse, under the date. (2) JEFFERSON NICKEL: on the reverse, at right of building or over dome. (3) WASHINGTON QUARTER: on the reverse, under the eagle. (4). MORGAN DOLLAR: on the reverse, under eagle. (5) BUFFALO NICKEL: on the reverse, under "five cents." (6) KENNEDY HALF DOLLAR: on the reverse, to the lower left of eagle. (7) MERCURY DIME: on the reverse, to left of fasces. (8) ROOSEVELT DIME: on the reverse, to left of torch base. (9) FRANKLIN HALF DOLLAR: on the reverse, over the bell. (10) LIBERTY STANDING HALF DOLLAR: on the reverse, on left side near edge. INDIAN HEAD CENTS: on the reverse, under wreath at bottom. LIBERTY SEATED DIMES: on the reverse, under wreath or within it. LIBERTY HEAD DIMES: on the reverse, under wreath. LIBERTY SEATED QUARTERS: on the reverse, under eagle. LIBERTY HEAD QUARTERS: on the reverse, under eagle. LIBERTY STANDING QUARTERS: on the obverse, above and to the left of the date. LIBERTY SEATED HALF DOLLARS: on the reverse, under eagle. LIBERTY HEAD HALF DOLLARS: on the reverse, to left of the words "half dollar." LIBERTY SEATED DOLLARS: on the reverse side, under the eagle.

STORING AND DISPLAYING YOUR COINS

Individual paper coin envelope and lucite tube for holding coins in rolls, by denomination

Coins can be used on bracelet and key chains. Dealers sell ring-shaped frames of silver or gold to fit coins of different sizes

A good collector treats coins with care and respect. They should be mounted and stored neatly, but in such a way that they can be readily taken out, studied, shown to friends, and so on. The right storing and handling can make a big difference in a coin's worth. If mishandled, the coin will become scratched or marred, and decrease in value. If kept properly, chances are that the coin will be worth more and more with each passing year.

In earlier times, coins were usually kept in small wax-paper envelopes, and removed for examining one at a time. Today there are many types of coin boards and albums with specially punched holes into which the coins fit snugly. Boards have been designed for all types of American coins, and many types of foreign coins as well. Some boards, or folders, have gummed paper in the cut-out circles to hold the coins in place. Others have round openings punched all the way through. In this way, when the coin is in place, both the obverse *and* the reverse side can be seen. Dates, mint marks, and other helpful information appear under each opening. Plastic strips slide into place to protect the coin's surfaces. Most boards have loose-leaf holes along one edge, so they can be assembled in book form.

Coins can also be mounted in individual lucite holders which show both sides. Some lucite holders are designed for special sets and commemorative issues. There are also tubes made of lucite to hold coins in rolls by denomination. Collectors can buy special rings for coins that are to be worn on bracelets or as pendants. Gold coins in particular make interesting jewelry, but coins should *never* be pierced. A coin with even a tiny hole drilled through it is a damaged coin. Instead, one of these thin metal rings, with a tiny clasp on top, makes it possible to hold a coin securely without defacing it in any way.

Every year, manufacturers put out new types of holders to help collectors do a better job of storage and display. But remember, it isn't necessary to spend a lot of money on equipment of this sort. All that is necessary is a type of mounting that will meet your needs simply, neatly, and efficiently.

CLEANING AND HANDLING

Most collectors believe that coins should never be cleaned, since this may spoil their surface or otherwise mar them. But sooner or later, every beginner gets an urge to do some cleaning, so it's best to know the right and wrong way. Silver coins can be cleaned with a paste made of baking soda and water. Rub the paste on with your fingers or a soft cloth. *Never* use a brush or scouring pad, and *never* use regular kitchen cleansers or silver polishes. After rubbing on the paste, wash it off with warm water. Dry with a blotter or facial tissue. Silver coins may also be washed in a mild solution of household ammonia and water, then dried as described.

Copper and bronze coins are very hard to clean. The finish can be ruined easily, making the coin worthless. The best way to clean one of these coins is to rub it gently with a little oil on a chamois cloth, which will take off surface dirt. But it's important to remember that *no* amount of washing or buffing will restore a coin to the luster it had when first minted.

Silver coins have a tendency to tarnish. Paper, except for special "tarnish-free" kinds, causes coins to tarnish faster, so coins should *not* be wrapped in ordinary papers. Rubber bands also cause tarnishing. If you lay a rubber band on a silver coin for a few days, you will notice that it leaves a black stripe on the coin when it is removed. To protect coins not mounted in boards or holders, wrap them in aluminum foil or cellophane and place them in tarnish-proof envelopes.

Care is also needed when coins are handled. A coin should always be picked up by its edges, rather than in the center, since handling can tarnish a coin. Some collectors even wear white cotton gloves when sorting and arranging their coins. Methods such as these may seem "fussy," but they can help greatly to maintain the beauty and value of a collection.

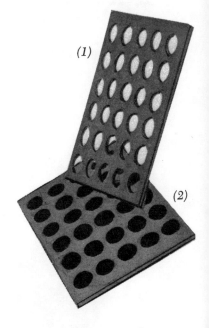

(1)

(2)

Two types of coin boards. The first holds sliding plastic strips, so both sides of the coin will show. The second has an adhesive backing to hold coins in place

Some coins are sold in their own special holders to protect them and to simplify display

55

COIN VALUES AND PRICES

The value of a coin depends chiefly on its *scarcity* and its *condition*. Rare coins are bound to be worth more than those that are plentiful. Coins in perfect condition are bound to be worth more than those that are scratched and worn. Needless to say, there must also be a *demand* for the coins.

In 1923, the Philadelphia mint turned out exactly 9,716,000 quarters. In the same year, the branch mint at San Francisco struck 1,360,000 of the same coins. As a result, the San Francisco quarters are scarcer. A regular Philadelphia-minted 1923 quarter in fine condition can be bought for about $6. The same coin with the San Francisco "S" mint mark costs about $65.

Many old coins are scarce today. Over the years coins are lost, or become worn out. Sometimes a vessel sinks, taking with it a large shipment of certain coins. Nobody knows how or where some coins have disappeared. In 1822, for instance, the Government minted 17,796 United States $5 gold pieces. Only three of these gold coins are known to exist at the present time. One is in the Smithsonian Institution, in Washington, D. C. The other two belong to private collectors. But no one knows what happened to all the rest. If one of these 1822 gold pieces should turn up, it will be worth thousands of dollars to the lucky owner.

During its operation, between 1837 and 1909, the New Orleans mint turned out many types of coins, but none in very large numbers. As a result, United States coins with an "O" mint mark are almost always worth more than the same coins minted elsewhere.

Proof coins are among the most interesting of all collectors' items. Produced from special dies, the result is a coin almost jewel-like in its polish and clarity. Proof coins are minted for collectors and as souvenirs. Proof *sets* consist of one of each type of United States coin in use. From 1936 to 1964 proof sets were produced each year at the Philadelphia mint and packaged in special cellophane envelopes, designed to keep

1804 cent, valued at over $500 if in fine condition

1804 dollar. A great rarity. Although many were issued, only thirteen are known to exist now. Collectors have paid thousands of dollars for these

1822 $5 gold piece. Only three of these coins are known to be in existence, though 17,796 were minted. These coins are so rare that no definite price can be estimated for one

1838 "O" half dollar. Because only twenty half dollars were minted in 1838 at the New Orleans plant, this is a valuable coin

them in spotless condition. For three years, they were not made. In 1968 production was resumed at the San Francisco mint, with the sets packaged in a rigid plastic holder. The face value of the coins adds up to 91¢, but they are always sold at a higher price. The 1969 charge for a proof set was $5.00. Proof sets can be bought from the United States Treasury Department. Collecting proof sets is becoming more and more popular, and they are going up steadily in value. In 1936, only 3,837 full proof sets were made. They sold at the time for $1.81. In 1970 this set cost almost $900. Here are other examples of proof set values:

Year Issued	Original Cost	1970 Cost
1937	$1.81	$365.00
1940	$1.81	$105.00
1955	$2.10	$ 30.00
1961	$2.10	$ 6.00

1894 "S" dime. In 1961, one of these coins was sold for $13,500

A typical proof set (1957, Philadelphia mint)

Extremely fine

Very fine

Fine

Just as important as scarcity is a coin's general appearance. Most things, from cars to coffee pots and from books to bicycles, are worth more if they are in good condition and show little "wear and tear." The same applies to coins. A collector can hold two Liberty Head dimes in his hand. Both are dated 1913, and both have the same San Francisco mint mark. But he can sell one of them for a dollar, and the other for ten times as much. The secret lies in the *condition* of the coins—how clearly the details and the lettering can be seen, and so on.

To help establish the exact condition of a coin, experts have created a set of grades which are used by all dealers and collectors. Here are these official classifications:

Proof: A coin with a mirrorlike surface, made with polished dies and a polished blank. *Proof* is the "de luxe" class of coin conditions. (Abbreviation: Pr.)

Uncirculated: A coin made for regular circulation, but not put into use. These are in perfect condition and show absolutely no signs of wear or damage. (Abbreviation: Unc.)

Extremely Fine: A coin that has been circulated, but shows only the slightest amount of wear. This class is also known as *Extra Fine.* (Abbreviation: Ex. F.)

Very Fine: A coin with slight wear, not quite as perfect as the class above, but still in excellent condition. (Abbreviation: V.F.)

Fine: A coin that has worn spots, but only on the high parts. Design and detail are still sharp. (Abbreviation: F.)

EXTREMELY FINE: Note, on the obverse, that the cheekbone is slightly worn, as are hairs at the temple and the bottom edge of the collar. On the reverse side, note that the base of the triangle above the four pillars shows weakly. VERY FINE: Obverse, the cheekbone and the hair at temple and collar's bottom edge are markedly worn. Reverse, the lines of the second pillar from the right are complete on both sides and not broken at the top or bottom. FINE: Obverse, further wearing of detail in the areas mentioned. Reverse, the second pillar shows, but is weak.

Good: A coin showing wear, but with the lettering and the design still plain. (Abbreviation: G.) Some dealers have a class between *Good* and *Fine* called *Very Good*.

Fair: A coin showing a great deal of wear, although it is still possible to recognize what the coin is. Coins in this class are not usually sought by collectors. (Abbreviation: Fr.) Coins worn almost smooth, or those which are damaged, are sometimes classed as *Poor*. These coins are worth face value only.

Part of the fun of collecting is to watch one's coins grow in worth over the years. Many coin catalogues are available that give the current value of every United States coin, past and present. Other catalogues give the prices of ancient and foreign coins. The collector should keep this information on hand. But remember that it's important to know whether the prices quoted are those a dealer will *pay* for a coin or those he himself will *charge* for it. The dealer has business expenses such as rent, advertising, salaries, and so on. He is also entitled to a fair profit. Because of this, he charges a good bit more for a particular coin than he will offer when he is buying it. Coins can also be sold and traded privately, to friends and to fellow collectors.

Of course, a serious hobbyist doesn't think of coin collecting as a gamble, or a "get rich quick" scheme. A real collector saves coins for pure enjoyment. If a collection increases in value, this can be looked upon as an extra "bonus" adding to the fun.

VERY GOOD: Note, on the obverse, that there is still more wear. On the reverse side, note that the second pillar is nearly gone, but the other pillars still show. GOOD: Obverse, there is still more wear, but the coin still has a good outer rim. Reverse, note that all four pillars are almost gone and the rim at the top is worn down almost to E PLURIBUS UNUM. FAIR: Obverse, the rim is worn down to the lettering. Reverse, the rim is worn down to the lettering on the edge. Note: the coins shown are not from the same sets. They were picked to best show grading differences.

Very good

Good

Fair

COLLECTING ANCIENT AND FOREIGN COINS

Foreign coins bring us closer to people of distant lands. They teach us geography and history. They show us places and events of yesterday, and bring the past to life.

A foreign coin collection usually starts with a handful of souvenirs brought back by someone traveling abroad. With this as a base, the collector can develop his collection in many different ways. Perhaps the simplest is to gather coins from as many different lands as possible, creating a United Nations of the coin world. Such a collection might contain pesos from Colombia, drachmas from Greece, rupees from India, prutahs from Israel, piastres from Morocco, rins from Japan, pesetas from Spain, and halalas from Yemen.

Not many holders are available for foreign coins, but with a little imagination, collectors can create their own methods of display. An assortment of ancient Greek and Roman coins, or Biblical coins, makes a fascinating exhibit when mounted on illustration board. Some collectors frame their prize items under glass, for use as a wall decoration.

An ambitious hobbyist might collect portrait coins of the Roman emperors. Every Roman ruler placed his image on the coinage of his time. Many of these are still available, and can be bought for $2 or less, depending on the coin's condition.

Here is a checklist of emperors whose portraits appear on Roman denarii, and the years during which they reigned.

Augustus (29 B.C. to A.D. 14)
Tiberius (A.D. 14 to A.D. 37)
Caligula (A.D. 37 to A.D. 41)
Claudius (A.D. 41 to A.D. 54)
Nero (A.D. 54 to A.D. 68)
Galba (A.D. 68 to A.D. 69)
Otho (A.D. 69)
Vitellius (A.D. 69)
Vespasian (A.D. 69 to A.D. 79)
Titus (A.D. 79 to A.D. 81)
Domitian (A.D. 81 to A.D. 96)
Nerva (A.D. 96 to A.D. 98)
Trajan (A.D. 98 to A.D. 117)
Hadrian (A.D. 117 to A.D. 138)
Antoninus Pius (A.D. 138 to 161)
Marcus Aurelius (A.D. 161 to A.D. 180)
Commodus (A.D. 180 to A.D. 192)
Pertinax (A.D. 193)
Didius Julianus (A.D. 193)

Pescennius Niger (A.D. 193 to A.D. 194)
Clodius Albinus (A.D. 193 to A.D. 197)
Septimius Severus (A.D. 193 to A.D. 211)
Caracalla (A.D. 211 to A.D. 217)
Geta (A.D. 209 to A.D. 212)
Macrinus (A.D. 217 to A.D. 218)
Elagabalus (A.D. 218 to A.D. 222)
Severus Alexander (A.D. 222 to A.D. 235)
Maximus I (A.D. 235 to A.D. 238)
Gordianus I (A.D. 238)
Gordianus II (A.D. 238)
Balbinus (A.D. 238)
Pupienus (A.D. 238)
Gordianus III (A.D. 238 to A.D. 244)
Philip I (A.D. 244 to A.D. 249)

Mexican centavo

Israeli prutah

Spanish Civil War peseta

Liberian half dollar

English guinea

Russian ruble

Later, emperors appear on bronze coins such as the *follis* and the *quinarius,* and on a silver-bronze coin called an *antoniniani.* Many rulers issued portrait coins showing their wives, children, and parents. These coins usually run higher in price, because they are scarcer.

Another interesting collection of portraits can be built around the kings and queens of England. From the time of King Henry VII, who reigned in the fifteenth century, every ruler appeared on English coins. Beginning with Queen Elizabeth I, the portrait of the ruler usually faced in an opposite direction to that of the person before. This became a regular pattern from the reign of Charles II on. Charles II was known as "the Merry Monarch." According to one theory, he so hated the gloomy atmosphere of the regime before him that he actually "turned his back" on it.

Charles II was also the first to issue "Maundy money." This was distributed to the poor every year on Maundy Thursday—the Thursday before Easter. A special set of small silver coins was made for the purpose, consisting of a penny, twopence, threepence, and fourpence. Distributing this "royal bounty" has become a British tradition. It is carried out each year, usually at Westminster Abbey. According to custom, the bounty is given to as many men and women as the monarch has years. The amount in each bounty bag also equals the king's age. A set of Maundy money coins is a fine addition to any collection of foreign pieces.

Because Canada is our neighbor, her coins have always been popular with American collectors. They are easier to obtain than most other foreign coins, and in parts of the northern United States are often accepted in trade. The first Canadian coins were issued by the province of Nova Scotia in 1817. Next came the province of Canada, issuing coins in 1858; then New Brunswick in 1861; and Newfoundland in 1865. When the Dominion of Canada was set up in 1870, Canada's official coinage was unified. Portraits of British rulers have always been featured on Canadian coins. The five rulers so honored are Victoria, Edward VII, George V, George VI, and Elizabeth II. Canadian coins currently in circulation are listed on the next page.

Small cent . . . . .first issued in 1920
Five-cent piece . . . . .first issued in 1922
Ten-cent piece . . . . .first issued in 1858
Twenty-five-cent piece . . . . .first issued in 1870
Fifty-cent piece . . . . .first issued in 1870
Silver dollar . . . . .first issued in 1935

*Twelve-sided nickel
from Canada*

Coin holders can be obtained for these Canadian pieces, as well as for other coins which are no longer in circulation.

An interesting sideline is the coinage of United States possessions such as the Virgin Islands, or the coins of Hawaii and Alaska before they became states.

In recent years, many new countries have come into being, such as Mali, Togo, and Pakistan. Some collectors specialize in saving coin sets issued by these new nations.

*Square five-cent piece
from Ceylon*

Other hobbyists collect coins on a geographic basis. One method is to draw an outline map of a particular area, such as South America or the Middle East, and to mount coins in the proper place for all the countries shown.

An interesting idea is to collect foreign coins with unusual shapes. In this group are the oblong *centavos* of the Mexican state of Oaxaca; the square coins of Malaya, Ceylon, and the Netherlands; and a twelve-sided threepence from England. Japan issues two oblong coins known as a *bu* and a *shu*. The *annas* of India are square, or round with wavy edges. Wavy, or scallop-edged, coins are also issued by Paraguay, Israel, Ghana, Ethiopia, and Cyprus.

*Square five tolas
from Bombay, India*

Another unusual collection can be built around coins with holes in their centers. We usually think of China and Japan in this connection, but many other countries now issue pierced coins. Among them are Norway, Greece, Lebanon, Belgium, Pakistan, France, Rhodesia, Nepal, Hungary, Nigeria, and the Fiji Islands.

Scallop-edged anna from India

Oblong centavo from Oaxaca, Mexico

63

Italian lire

Japanese sen

Norwegian ore

French franc

COINS AROUND THE WORLD

Portuguese escudo

Spanish peseta

From time to time, many countries change their coin designs. Some nations, such as France, have changed their coinage to keep step with history. At first, French coins showed portraits of French kings. Next came symbols of the French Revolution, and the famous slogan "Liberty, Equality, Fraternity." When Napoleon was made emperor, his portraits adorned the franc. Today, France's coins once again have designs symbolizing the Republic.

Although coin designs may change, the type of coin often stays the same. The following chart lists many countries of our modern world and examples of the types of coins they are using.

COUNTRY	COINS IN USE
Afghanistan	Puls, Afghani, Rupee
Angola	Escudo, Centavo, Macuta
Argentina	Peso, Centavo
Australia	Cent
Austria	Krone, Heller, Schilling, Groschen
Belgium	Franc, Centime
Bolivia	Boliviano, Centavo
Brazil	Milreis, Reis
Bulgaria	Leva, Stotinki
Burma	Kyat, Pyas, Anna
Canada	Dollar, Cent
Chile	Condor, Peso, Centavo
China	Dollar, Cent, Cash
Colombia	Peso, Centavo
Costa Rica	Colon, Centimo, Centavo
Cuba	Peso, Centavo
Czechoslovakia	Korona, Haleru
Denmark	Krone, Ore
Dominican Republic	Peso, Centavo
Ecuador	Condor, Sucre, Centavo
Egypt	Millieme, Piastre, Guerche
El Salvador	Peso, Colon, Centavo
Ethiopia	Talari, Guerche, Matonas
Finland	Markka, Penni
France	Franc, Centime
Germany	Mark, Pfennig
Ghana	Pesewa
Great Britain	Half Crown, Shilling, Pence, Penny
Greece	Drachma, Lepta
Guatemala	Peso, Quetzal, Reale, Centavo
Haiti	Gourde, Cent
Honduras	Peso, Centavo
Hungary	Pengo, Filler
Iceland	Krona, Aurar

Afghanistan afghani

Russian kopeck

German pfenning, Western Zone

German mark, Eastern Zone

Mexican peso

Turkish piastre

COUNTRY	COINS IN USE
India	Rupee, Anna, Pie, Pice
Iran (Persia)	Pahlevi, Rial, Dinar
Iraq	Dinar, Riyal, Dirhem, Fils
Ireland	Florin, Shilling, Pence
Israel	Prutah
Italy	Lira, Centesimi
Japan	Yen, Sen, Rin
Jordan	Fil, Fils, Dinar
Korea	Won, Chon, Fun, Yang
Lebanon	Lira, Piastre
Liberia	Dollar, Cent
Libya	Millieme, Piastre
Mexico	Peso, Centavo
Morocco	Ryal, Piastre, Mazunas
Mozambique	Escudo, Centavo
Netherlands	Guilder, Cent
New Zealand	Florin, Shilling, Pence
Nicaragua	Cordoba, Centavo
Nigeria	Shilling, Pence
Norway	Krone, Ore
Pakistan	Rupee, Anna, Pie, Pice
Panama	Balboa, Centesimo
Paraguay	Peso, Centavo, Centimo
Peru	Sol, Libra, Dinero, Centavo
Philippines	Peso, Centavo
Poland	Zloty, Croszy
Portugal	Escudo, Centavo
Rhodesia	Florin, Shilling, Pence
Romania	Leu, Bani
Saudi Arabia	Riyal, Girsh Miri, Girsh Darij
Spain	Peseta, Centimo
Sweden	Krona, Ore
Switzerland	Franc, Centime, Rappen
Syria	Lira, Piastre
Thailand	Tical, Att, Satang
Togo	Franc, Centime
Tunisia	Franc, Centime
Turkey	Lira, Piastre, Para
USSR (Russia)	Ruble, Kopeck
Uruguay	Peso, Centesimo
Vatican City	Lira, Centesimi
Venezuela	Bolivar, Centimo
Vietnam	Dong, Piastre, Hao, Xu
Yemen	Imadi, Guerche, Bogach, Halala
Yugoslavia	Dinar, Para

An interesting bracelet composed of U.S.
gold coins. The face value of the coins is under $50,
but the actual market value would be over $400

COLLECTING AMERICAN COINS

Most collectors concentrate on coins of the country in which they live. The reason is simple: coins of our own country are the most plentiful and the easiest to get. They pass through our hands day after day, in the form of small change, allowance, and so on. We also have friends, relatives, and local shopkeepers who can help in the never-ending hunt for missing dates and items.

American coins have always been popular collectors' items. They can be collected chiefly in two ways: by *series* and by *type*.

COLLECTING BY SERIES

This is a good way to begin collecting coins. The object is to obtain a complete series of certain coins, getting one coin of *each date* from *each mint* where it was made. A typical series, for example, is the Indian Head nickel, also known as the Buffalo nickel. This series was issued from 1913 through 1938. It was minted at Philadelphia, San Francisco, and Denver. The mint marks for San Francisco (S) and Denver (D) can be found under the words FIVE CENTS, below the design of the buffalo on the reverse side. Those minted at Philadelphia show *no* mint mark. The series collector tries to get *one of each* of these many nickels. Some can be found in change, or bought from dealers for a small sum. Others are harder to get. Among these are the 1913 and 1921 nickels with the mint mark S, and those of 1913 and 1924 with the mint mark D.

Ancient Roman coin (43-31 B.C.)

Estonian kroon

COLLECTING BY TYPE

This is easier for more advanced collectors, since it includes old coins which are scarce and therefore expensive. The object is to obtain one coin of every *design* that has been issued. Any date or mint will do. There are, for example, ten different types of cent pieces which have been issued at various times by the United States. These go from the Chain cent, minted in 1793, to the Lincoln Head cent, which is being made at the present time. The type collector tries to get *one of each* of these ten designs. The same can be done with nickels, dimes, quarters, and all other American coins.

Of course, there are no strict rules or "musts." It's possible to collect both series *and* types, or to specialize in certain years and subjects. Some people build collections around events in American history. Often a particular theme will lead to broader areas, such as the collection of ship coins shown here.

Today, there are all kinds of coin folders, albums, and plastic holders made for both series and type collectors. These contain dates and other helpful information. Another big help is the

Chinese dollar

English half penny

Canadian ten-cent piece

use of names to identify our various coin types and designs. For example, the goddess of Liberty appears on many coins. These are known as "Liberty Seated," "Liberty Standing," "Liberty Head," "Liberty Cap," "Winged Head Liberty," and so on. On some early coins the head of Liberty includes the bust and shoulders. These are known as the "Bust" and "Draped Bust." Some Liberty cents are known by the way the lady wears her hair—"Braided Hair," "Turban Head," and "Coronet."

Besides names, coins sometimes have nicknames. The dimes, quarters, and half dollars of the 1892-1916 issue were designed by mint engraver Charles E. Barber. As a result, they are often called "Barber Head" coins. Silver dollars of the 1878-1921 issue were designed by mint engraver George T. Morgan, and are known as "Morgan" dollars. The Braided Hair cent of 1839 is sometimes called the "Booby Head" cent, because of the absent-minded look on Miss Liberty's face!

On the following pages you will find a listing of all officially minted United States coins and the years in which they were produced.

Canadian dollar

Liberty Cap half cent

Draped Bust half cent

Turban Head half cent

HALF CENT

Braided Hair half cent

This coin was minted, on and off, between 1793 and 1857. Though not in circulation today, half-cent pieces are still found in attics, basements, and old trunks. They were made of copper, and have no mint marks. Types and years minted:

Liberty Cap 1793-1797
Draped Bust 1800-1808
Turban Head 1809-1836
Braided Hair 1840-1857

Chain cent

Wreath cent

CENT

Liberty Cap cent

This is our well known "penny." At first, *large* cents were minted, about the size of a modern quarter. But the large size was costly and impractical. In 1857 it was replaced by a *small* cent, similar to the one now used. These were first made of a mixture, or alloy, of copper and nickel. Later, they were minted of copper, tin, and zinc. In 1943, to save precious metal for the war effort, the cent was made of steel. Today they are again a copper alloy. The Indian Head cent, issued from 1859 to 1909, is one of the most popular items in coin collecting. The Lincoln Head cent now in use was first minted in 1909, to celebrate the 100th anniversary of Abraham Lincoln's birth. The

Draped Bust Cent

Turban Head cent

Coronet cent

coin was produced at the Philadelphia, Denver, and San Francisco mints. Mint marks for Denver (D) and San Francisco (S) appear just below the date. A small number of 1909 cents carried the designer's initials—VDB. These were dropped, but put back again in 1918. Cents dated 1909 carrying the VDB letters are rare and valuable. In 1959, a new reverse side was designed by Frank Gasparro, to mark the 150th anniversary of Lincoln's birth. The new reverse shows the Lincoln Memorial in Washington, D. C. Types and years minted:

Braided Hair cent

LARGE CENTS

Chain 1793
Wreath 1793
Liberty Cap 1793-1796
Draped Bust 1796-1807
Turban Head 1808-1814
Coronet 1816-1839
Braided Hair 1839-1857

SMALL CENTS

Flying Eagle 1856-1858
Indian Head 1859-1909
Lincoln Head . . . . .1909 to the present

Flying Eagle cent

Indian Head cent

Lincoln Head cent

TWO-CENT PIECE

This bronze coin had a short life of only nine years. Though it was not popular, the two-cent piece has a very important place in the history of American coinage—it was the first of our coins to bear the famed motto "In God We Trust." The only type minted was the Shield design. This was first issued in 1864, and discontinued in 1873. In 1873, only proof copies were made.

Two-cent piece

Star three-cent piece

Liberty Head three-cent piece

Liberty Flowing Hair half dime

Draped Bust half dime

Shield nickel

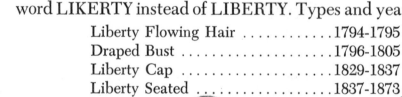

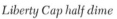

Liberty Head nickel

THREE-CENT PIECE

This coin was first issued in 1851. There are two different types. The first was made of silver and was the smallest coin ever issued by the United States, even smaller than our present dime. In 1865, the coin was issued in a larger size. This was made of a blend of nickel, copper, and zinc. The three-cent piece was never successful and was discontinued in 1889. Types and years minted:

Star (silver) 1851-1873
Liberty Head (nickel) 1865-1889

HALF DIME

This was minted from 1794 to 1805. The coin was again issued in 1829 and continued through 1873, when it was finally dropped. Half dimes were made of silver. Many have the New Orleans (O) mint mark on the reverse, near the bottom of the wreath. From 1863 to 1873, the San Francisco mint also produced half dimes. Its mint mark appears in the same spot. Because of a broken die, some of the 1796 half dimes show the word LIKERTY instead of LIBERTY. Types and years minted:

Liberty Flowing Hair 1794-1795
Draped Bust 1796-1805
Liberty Cap 1829-1837
Liberty Seated 1837-1873

Liberty Cap half dime

Liberty Seated half dime

NICKEL

This coin, our well known five-cent piece, is actually a blend of nickel and copper. It was first issued after the Civil War, to take the place of the half dime and of fractional paper money then being used. One of the most popular types is the Indian Head nickel, with the buffalo on the reverse. This was minted between 1913 and 1938, and many are still in circulation. The first of these coins showed the buffalo standing on a mound. After 1913, the design was changed to show the buffalo standing on level ground. The Jefferson nickel, now being minted, shows America's third president. On the reverse side is a view of Monticello, the beautiful home which Jefferson himself designed. The Jefferson nickel was created by Felix Schlag, and was the first coin design to be chosen in a free, open competition. During World War II, to save nickel, five-cent pieces were made of a blend of copper, silver, and manganese. To set these coins apart, the Philadelphia mint put a special mint mark—a large P—over the dome of the building on the reverse. This is the only time a Philadelphia mint mark has been shown on a United States coin. In 1946, use of the regular nickel alloy was resumed. Types and years minted:

Indian Head nickel

Shield 1866-1883
Liberty Head 1883-1912
Indian Head (or Buffalo) 1913-1938
Jefferson ....1938 to the present

Jefferson nickel

 *Bust dime*   *Liberty Seated dime*

DIME

This is the smallest United States coin now in circulation, and was once spelled "disme." It was first issued in 1796. At various times it has been minted at Philadelphia, Denver, New Orleans, San Francisco, and Carson City, Nevada. The Winged Head Liberty dime, minted from 1916 to 1945, is also known as the Mercury dime because it looks so much like Mercury, the Roman god of speed and commerce. Many of these are still in circulation. The Roosevelt dime first appeared in 1946, and is still being made. It shows our thirty-second president, and was designed by John R. Sinnock. Roosevelt dime mint marks (S and D) can be found on the reverse, just to the left of the torch, near the bottom. In 1955, there were far fewer of these dimes made than usual. So dimes of this date are becoming scarce and will grow in value. Types and years minted:

Liberty Head dime

Winged Head Liberty dime

Bust 1796-1837
Liberty Seated 1837-1891
Liberty Head (Barber) 1892-1916
Winged Head Liberty (or Mercury) 1916-1945
Roosevelt ....1946 to the present

Roosevelt dime

73

Twenty-cent piece

TWENTY-CENT PIECE

This coin had a very short and unsuccessful life. It was first minted in 1875, but its size was so close to the size of a quarter that it caused great confusion. The coin was discontinued in 1878. The only type minted was the Liberty Seated design. It appeared in 1875 and 1876. In 1877 and 1878 only proof copies were made.

Liberty Seated quarter

Bust quarter

Liberty Head quarter

QUARTER

This coin is so named because it is worth twenty-five cents, or a quarter of one dollar. Quarters were introduced in 1796. They have been made at the New Orleans, Carson City, San Francisco, Denver, and Philadelphia mints. On all types, except Liberty Standing, mint marks can be found on the reverse, just below the eagle. On the Liberty Standing quarter, the mint mark is on the obverse side, to the left and slightly above the date. The Liberty Head quarter issued from 1892 to 1916 is also known as the Barber quarter, like its cousins, the Barber dime and Barber half dollar. The quarter now being minted was issued in honor of the 200th birthday of George Washington. It was designed by John Flanagan. Types and years minted:

Liberty Standing quarter

Washington quarter

Bust 1796-1838
Liberty Seated 1838-1891
Liberty Head (Barber) 1892-1916
Liberty Standing. 1916-1930
Washington .1932 to the present

Bust half dollar

Liberty Seated half dollar

HALF DOLLAR

This coin, our fifty-cent piece, was first minted in Philadelphia in 1794. Until 1838 all half dollars were made at the Philadelphia mint, so they do not show mint marks. Since then, the coins have also been made at San Francisco, Carson City, and Denver. These mint marks can be found on the reverse, just below the eagle. Our present fifty-cent piece is the Kennedy half dollar, issued in honor of our thirty-fifth president. This coin carries a likeness of John F. Kennedy sculptured by Gilroy Roberts, chief engraver of the United States Mint. The reverse side of the coin shows the Presidential coat of arms. Types and years minted:

Bust 1794-1839
Liberty Seated 1839-1891
Liberty Head (Barber) 1892-1915
Liberty Standing...............1916-1947
Franklin 1948-1963
Kennedy ....1964 to the present

Liberty Head half dollar

Liberty Standing half dollar

Franklin half dollar

Kennedy half dollar

Bust dollar

Liberty Seated dollar

SILVER DOLLAR

This is the grandfather of all United States coins in everyday use. Most people prefer carrying dollar bills made of paper, but silver dollars are very popular in our western and Midwestern states. These coins were minted from 1794 to 1935. At first, silver dollars carried lettering around the edges. From 1840 on, they were issued with a regular reeded edge, as on other coins. All silver dollars carry a Liberty design on the obverse side. Mint marks can be found on the reverse, just below the eagle or wreath, or, on the Peace dollar, just above the rear tip of the eagle's wing. This coin was so named because it was issued to celebrate the ending of World War I. Types and years minted:

Bust	1794-1839
Liberty Seated	1840-1873
Liberty Head (Morgan)	1878-1921
Peace	1921-1935

Liberty Head dollar

Peace dollar

TRADE DOLLAR

This silver coin was minted from 1873 to 1885, at the Philadelphia, San Francisco, and Carson City mints. The coin was created to help our merchants in trading with the Orient. Since they were used mostly in China, many are marked with Chinese symbols stamped on by Chinese banks. Trade dollars, though an interesting collector's item, are no longer valid. They are the only United States coins which cannot be used as money. The only type minted was the Liberty Seated design. It was issued from 1873 to 1878. From 1879 to 1885, only proof copies were made. These are very valuable today.

Trade dollar (1877)

Trade dollar (1873)

When collectors check the coins which come their way each day, there's always the chance of making a lucky find—discovering one or two which are worth a good bit more than their face value. Here is a checklist of United States coins in the current series which are the *most valuable* of their type:

Lincoln Head Cents 1909 (S); 1909 (S)VDB; 1911 (S); 1912 (S); 1914 (D); 1914 (S); 1921 (S); 1923 (S); 1924 (D); 1924 (S); 1926 (S); 1931 (S); 1933 (D).
Jefferson Nickels 1939 (D); 1939 (S); 1942 (D).
Roosevelt Dimes 1949 (S); 1950 (S); 1951 (S); 1952 (S).
Washington Quarters 1932 (D); 1932 (S); 1936 (D).
Franklin Half Dollars 1948; 1949; 1950.

COLLECTING AMERICAN COMMEMORATIVE COINS

Isabella commemorative

Since early times, coins have been used to honor important events and famous people. These memorial pieces are known as commemorative coins. Sometimes they are sold at a special price, and the money is used to pay for a celebration or a monument.

Commemorative coins of America are among the most beautiful coins issued anywhere. Commemoratives must be authorized by a special act of Congress. The very first one was a silver half dollar, issued in 1892 to honor Christopher Columbus. Next came a silver quarter with a portrait of Queen Isabella

Oregon Trail Memorial commemorative

Pilgrim Tercentenary commemorative

of Spain, who helped finance Columbus' voyage to the new world. This was the first American coin to show the image of a foreign monarch. The third commemorative coin issued by the United States was the Lafayette dollar. This coin honored the French general who helped the colonies during the American Revolution.

In all, more than fifty commemorative coins have been issued by the United States. Most are silver half dollars. Hobbyists who collect these unusual pieces can learn much about the highlights of American history.

Lexington-Concord Sesquicentennial commemorative

Lafayette commemorative

Silver Commemoratives (all are half dollars, except for the Isabella and Lafayette coins)

Columbian Exposition 1892, 1893
Isabella Quarter 1893
Lafayette Dollar 1900
Panama-Pacific Exposition 1915
Illinois Centennial 1918
Maine Centennial 1920
Pilgrim Tercentenary 1920, 1921
Missouri Centennial 1921
Alabama Centennial 1921
Grant Memorial 1922
Monroe Doctrine Centennial 1923
Huguenot-Walloon Tercentenary 1924
Lexington-Concord Sesquicentennial 1925
Stone Mountain Memorial 1925
California Diamond Jubilee 1925
Fort Vancouver Centennial 1925
Sesquicentennial of American Independence 1926
Oregon Trail Memorial 1926, 1928, 1933,
                                           1934, 1936-1939
Vermont Sesquicentennial 1927
Hawaiian Sesquicentennial 1928
Maryland Tercentenary 1934
Texas Centennial 1934-1938
Daniel Boone Bicentennial 1934-1938
Connecticut Tercentenary 1935
Arkansas Centennial 1935-1939
Hudson, New York, Sesquicentennial 1935
California-Pacific Exposition 1935, 1936
Old Spanish Trail 1935
Providence, Rhode Island, Tercentenary 1936
Cleveland Great Lakes Exposition 1936
Wisconsin Territorial Centennial 1936
Cincinnati Musical Center 1936
Long Island Tercentenary 1936

Hawaiian Sesquicentennial commemorative

York County, Maine, Tercentenary 1936
Bridgeport, Connecticut, Centennial 1936
Lynchburg, Virginia, Sesquicentennial 1936
Elgin, Illinois, Centennial .1936
Albany, New York, Charter 1936
San Francisco-Oakland Bay Bridge 1936
Columbia, South Carolina, Sesquicentennial 1936
Arkansas Centennial (Sen. Robinson) 1936
Delaware Tercentenary 1936
Battle of Gettysburg 1936
Norfolk, Virginia, Bicentennial 1936
Roanoke Island, North Carolina 1937
Battle of Antietam 1937
New Rochelle, New York .1938
Iowa Centennial 1946
Booker T. Washington Memorial 1946-1951
George Washington Carver 1951-1954

Gold Commemoratives (dollars, except for the Panama-Pacific
and Philadelphia Sesquicentennial coins)

Louisiana Purchase Exposition
 (Jefferson Head) 1903
Louisiana Purchase Exposition
 (McKinley Head) 1903
Lewis and Clark Centennial 1904, 1905
Panama-Pacific Exposition ($1) 1915
Panama-Pacific Exposition
 ($2.50) 1915
Panama-Pacific Exposition
 ($50 round) 1915
Panama-Pacific Exposition
 ($50 octagonal) 1915
McKinley Memorial 1916, 1917
Grant Memorial 1922
Philadelphia Sesquicentennial
 ($2.50) 1926

Battle of Gettysburg
commemorative

Lewis and Clark Centennial
commemorative

COLLECTING AMERICAN
GOLD PIECES

U.S. $5 gold piece

Gold is one of the oldest and most beautiful of all metals. It is also one of the most valuable. The pursuit of this precious substance has carried men to every corner of the globe, from the icy wastes of Alaska to the steaming jungles of the Congo. Ancient kings fought bloody wars for gold. Emperors sent huge fleets to colonize distant lands in the hope of finding gold there. No metal has ever had a more colorful or a more dramatic history.

The first gold coins minted for the United States Government were half eagles, valued at $5 each and issued in 1795. All American gold coins were taken out of regular circulation in 1933. But America's gold reserves, stored at Fort Knox, are still used to back up our currency.

Because they have been out of production and circulation for so long, United States gold pieces have steadily gone up in value. They are too expensive for most hobbyists to save in quantity, but a few good samples can add interest to any collection.

On the following page you will find a listing of all officially minted United States gold coins, and the years in which they were issued. The list includes all gold pieces except commemorative coins.

Since early times, gold has been recognized as one of the most precious of all metals. It has been used in coinage in every part of the globe

*Liberty Head
Gold Dollar*

*Coronet Type
Quarter Eagle ($2.50)*

*Indian Headdress
$3 Gold Piece*

*Flowing Hair
$4 Gold Piece*

*Liberty Head
Half Eagle ($5)*

*Indian Head
Eagle ($10)*

GOLD DOLLAR

Liberty Head	1849-1854
Indian Headdress	1854-1856
Indian Headdress (larger design)	1856-1889

QUARTER EAGLE ($2.50)

Liberty Cap	1796-1807
Liberty Head	1808-1834
Ribbon Type	1834-1839
Coronet Type	1840-1907
Indian Head	1908-1929

THREE-DOLLAR GOLD PIECE

Indian Headdress	1854-1889

FOUR-DOLLAR GOLD PIECE (Proofs only)

Flowing Hair	1879-1880
Coiled Hair	1879-1880

HALF EAGLE ($5.00)

Liberty Head	1795-1807
Liberty Facing Left	1807-1834
Ribbon Type	1834-1838
Coronet Type	1839-1908
Indian Head	1908-1929

EAGLE ($10.00)

Liberty Head	1795-1804
Coronet Type	1838-1907
Indian Head	1907-1933

DOUBLE EAGLE ($20.00)

Coronet Type	1849-1907
Liberty Standing	1907-1933

The $20 Liberty Standing gold piece was designed by the famed sculptor Augustus Saint-Gaudens. It is considered one of the most beautiful coins ever produced in America. The obverse shows Miss Liberty holding a torch in her right hand and an olive branch in her left. The reverse shows an American eagle in full flight, outlined against the rays of the sun.

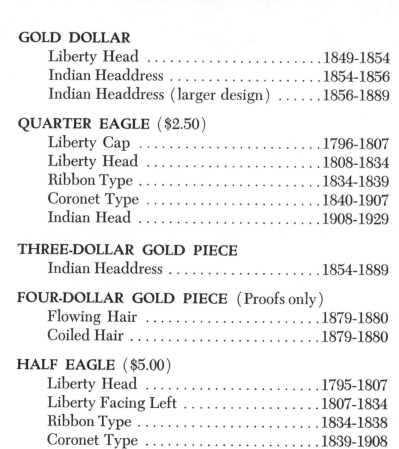

*Liberty Standing Double Eagle ($20)
designed by Augustus Saint-Gaudens and
considered one of the most beautiful
coins ever produced in America*

84

COLLECTING "FREAKS" AND SPECIALTIES

Machines, like people, sometimes make mistakes. In the production of coins, a die may break, a feed-belt slip, or a stamping device miss a few strokes. The result is a coin, or group of coins, with faulty designs. These are known as mint errors, or "freaks." Since they are quite rare, mint errors are valuable, and collectors enjoy hunting them.

A spelling error: "inited" for "united" on an 1801 cent

The most unusual "freak" occurs when the wrong metal is used. If, for example, a silver planchet is accidentally mixed with a stack of copper planchets, the result will be a silver one-cent coin. These pieces are known as *off metal* coins. Sometimes a planchet is struck twice, and both impressions are visible. These are called *double struck* coins. *Off center* coins are produced when the planchets aren't properly lined up between the dies. Usually, the farther off center such a coin is struck, the more valuable it becomes.

1883 nickel without "CENTS"

Triple-struck 1863 Indian Head cent

One of the most recent mint errors is the 1955 double die Lincoln cent, also known as the "shift" penny. On the obverse, everything except Lincoln's profile appears in double—there are two dates, two legends, and so on. These coins sell at present for about $165. Some are still in circulation and can be found in change, especially in the New England area.

Double-struck penny

An interesting mint error happened at Denver in 1937. One of the dies broke while stamping out nickels. As a result, the buffalo on these coins lost his right foreleg. Some of these

Three-legged 1937 "D" Buffalo nickel

The famous 1955 "shift" penny

An off-center coin (1951 cent)

Advertising token

Scrip coupon—
50c Piggly Wiggly Script
(1933, Jonesboro, Arkansas)

Colonial token

Alaskan token

"three-legged" 1937 (D) buffalo nickels are still in circulation. A clear, sharp specimen is worth more than $40.

Another well known mint error concerns the 1918 silver quarters minted at San Francisco. Some of these have an "over-strike" on the date—the numeral 8 has been stamped over the numeral 7, and both numbers are visible. A regular 1918 San Francisco mint quarter in good condition is worth about $4. The same quarter with the "8 over 7" error is worth $150!

In addition to mint errors, there are other sidelines, or "specialties," of interest to coin fanciers. Among these special collectors' items are:

Territorial gold coins	Confederate coins
"Hard times" tokens	Civil War tokens
Advertising coins	Fractional currency
Subway and bus tokens	Souvenir medals
Encased postage stamps	Military decorations
Colonial money	Hawaiian and Alaskan tokens

A special set of Alaskan tokens was issued by the United States Government in 1935, for use by settlers in the Matanuska Valley. These colorful pieces were called "bingles." Stamped on them were legends such as "Good for $1 in trade," "Good for 20 cents in merchandise," and "Good for one drink."

Only two coins were designed for the Confederate States of America. These were a silver half dollar, and a cent which was struck in gold, silver, copper, and a copper-nickel alloy. Since there was very little metal on hand in the Confederacy, only proof copies of these coins were made. Today they are extremely rare and valuable.

Just the opposite is true of the Civil War tokens issued by the North. Because official United States copper cents were scarce, token cent pieces were issued by private firms and individuals. These were made either of nickel, copper, silver, or brass. It is believed that as many as 50,000,000 private tokens were struck, in 10,000 different types and styles. Because of this huge quantity, many Civil War tokens are still available. They can be purchased from dealers for as little as fifty cents each.

Souvenir medals, like commemorative coins, are issued to honor a famous person or event. Large sized medals are called medallions. However, unlike commemorative coins, *medals and medallions cannot be used as regular money.* They are strictly for decorative and souvenir use, and are issued by government or private organizations, committees, jewelry companies, and so on.

A good example is a recent medallion issued by the Dag Hammarskjöld Foundation honoring the late Secretary-General of the United Nations. The obverse shows a portrait of Mr. Hammarskjöld and the dates 1905-1961. The reverse carries the United Nations seal. Medals such as this make an interesting sideline project for many coin collectors.

Susan B. Anthony medal from the Hall of Fame series

Dag Hammarskjöld medallion issued to honor the famed Secretary-General of the United Nations

COUNTERFEIT COINS

"This yere, in Februarie, a woman had been seized in Smithfield for clipping of gold, but the kynge's pardon came, she being at the stake ready to be burnte."

Obverse and reverse of a 1652 Pine Tree shilling that shows excessive clipping

Clipped Pine Tree Shilling

Clipped Pine Tree Shilling

In ancient times, counterfeiters shaved or clipped the edges of coins to get extra metal. The above account, from an English law record of King Henry VIII, tells of a woman who was almost burned at the stake for doing this. Penalties in those days were very severe, not only for clipping coins, but for all types of counterfeiting.

The word "counterfeit" comes from the Latin *contra*, which means against, or the wrong way; and *facio*, which means to make. Counterfeit money is indeed money "made the wrong way." It is a practice almost as old as money itself.

In the days of ancient Greece and Rome, makers of false coins were already at work. Near the English town of Halton Chesters are the ruins of an old Roman fort. Among these ruins are the remains of a Roman counterfeiter's den. Here, 1,600 years ago, a forger and his gang made fake coins, passing them off on Roman troops and the local populace.

During the Middle Ages, counterfeiting was so widespread that the authorities were unable to control it. They decreed the severest punishments, including hanging and burning at the stake. In China, counterfeiters were beheaded. But the practice went on, and counterfeiters became bolder. During the sixteenth century a notorious gang of German forgers lived and worked in France, completely safe from arrest. In return for this protection, they promised their French rulers that they would only forge German and Austrian coins!

With the coming of machinery, coin counterfeiting gradually declined. Counterfeiters today are more interested in paper money than in metal pieces. For one thing, the invention of the reeded edge makes it impossible to clip or shave coins, because this can easily be noticed. And coins produced by modern machines are so well made that they can't be easily or cheaply faked. However, there are always *some* counterfeit coins around. The United States Secret Service suggests these dependable ways of spotting them:

- Counterfeit coins are usually greasy, or "soapy," to the touch
- When dropped, counterfeits sound dull, while genuine coins have a bell-like ring
- Counterfeit coins can often be cut with a knife; with genuine coins this is very difficult or impossible
- The reeding, or corrugation, on the edge of a counterfeit coin is usually rough and faulty, while on a genuine coin it is even and regular

There is another kind of counterfeiting of special concern to collectors. This is the doctoring, or changing, of ordinary coins to make them seem rare and valuable.

The 1804 cent, for example, is quite rare. Forgers have tried to create some of these by taking cents dated 1801, and turning the "1" into a "4." Another example is the rare 1914 Lincoln Head cent minted in Denver. Counterfeiters have faked this by taking a 1944 (D) cent and engraving out *part* of the first "4" to make it look like a "1." The result is a very good copy of the 1914 date—except that there is too much space between the "9" and the "14."

When buying rare coins, collectors must at all times use care, caution, and sharp eyes. Counterfeits such as those described can be spotted by scratch marks, uneven letters, or improper gaps between the numerals.

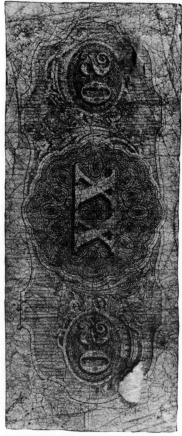

Counterfeiters practise their skills on paper money as well as coins. Shown here is a counterfeit Confederate $20 bill

PAST, PRESENT, AND FUTURE

Thousands of years have gone by since people like Chimgawa and Nekondeg used barter to get what they wanted. Since those primitive days, mankind has become civilized. The record of this amazing change is called history, and much of it can be traced through our coinage and currency. Coins are like links in a great, historic chain. Here is a group of coins which represent some of these outstanding links, and the people who helped to forge them:

THE DARIC OF ARTAXERXES

This coin was used during the reign of Artaxerxes I, king of ancient Persia from 465 B.C. to 425 B.C. At that time, the Persian Empire was a mighty domain which stretched over vast lands including Babylonia, Assyria, Cyprus, and parts of Egypt. The daric was made of pure gold. It usually showed a bearded king on the obverse. He carried a bow, which was the national weapon of ancient Persia.

THE TETRADRACHM OF ALEXANDER

This coin was used in the time of Alexander the Great, who lived from 356 B.C. to 323 B.C. Alexander was the son of King Philip of Macedon. He died at the age of 33, but during his short life, he ruled over millions of people. Alexander spread Greek learning to almost every part of the then known world. The tetradrachm was a favorite coin of the Alexandrian era.

THE AUREUS OF JULIUS CAESAR

This coin was used during the reign of Julius Caesar, the renowned general who became ruler of the Roman Empire. Caesar lived from 102 B.C. to 44 B.C. Under his command, Rome's armies made conquests in Spain, Syria, Gaul, Africa, Asia, even in far-off England. The aureus was introduced by Caesar himself. It was the most important Roman gold coin for hundreds of years.

91

THE DENARIUS OF NERO

This coin was popular during the time of Nero, emperor of Rome from A.D. 54 to A.D. 68. Nero was a tyrant and a despot. He was the first of the Roman rulers to persecute Christians. During his rule, in the year A.D. 64, Rome caught on fire. According to legend, Nero played the lyre while the city burned. The denarius was the main silver coin of those times.

THE FOLLIS OF CONSTANTINE

This coin was used in the reign of Emperor Constantine I, also known as Constantine the Great. He lived from A.D. 288 to A.D. 337. Constantine was the first Roman ruler to adopt Christianity, and to give the new Christian faith his imperial support and protection. The bronze follis was a popular coin throughout the Constantinian period.

THE SOLIDUS OF JUSTINIAN

This coin was popular in the time of Justinian I, Byzantine emperor from A.D. 527 to A.D. 565. Justinian's great domain stretched over Asia, Africa, and Italy. Its capital was the city of Constantinople. Justinian helped greatly to improve and spread the Roman code of law. The solidus was made of gold, and became the main coin of early Europe. It survived for 1,000 years, until the end of the Byzantine Empire.

THE DENIER OF CHARLEMAGNE

This coin was used in the reign of Charlemagne, or Charles the Great, king of the Franks from A.D. 768 to A.D. 814. His rule covered much of Europe, including the country now called France. Charlemagne gave land to his followers, established fair laws, and promoted the building of schools and monasteries. The denier, made of silver, took its name from the Roman denarius. It was the chief European silver coin of that era.

THE AUGUSTALIS OF FREDERICK

This coin was popular at the time of Frederick II, who governed Lombardy, Germany, and Sicily. He lived from 1194 to 1250, during the time of the Crusades. King Frederick was one of the great rulers of the Middle Ages. He promoted farming and industry. He was a fine artist, scientist, and poet. He was also interested in medicine and astronomy. The augustalis was made of gold, and was typical of the coinage of that period.

THE CROWN OF ELIZABETH

This coin was used in the time of Queen Elizabeth I of England, who reigned from 1558 to 1603. Elizabeth was the daughter of Henry VIII and Ann Boleyn. It was during her rule that Sir Francis Drake defeated the great Spanish Armada, making England the world's strongest sea power. The crown was first struck during the reign of Elizabeth's father. It was issued as a gold coin. Later a silver crown was also issued.

THE ECU OF LOUIS XIV

This coin, in varied forms, has been a part of French history for centuries. During the reign of Louis XIV, from 1643 to 1715, it was issued as a large silver piece. This period was the golden age of French art, music, and literature. It was during his reign that the magnificent Palace of Versailles was built. *Ecu* is the French word for "shield." The coin had the same importance as the English crown and the American dollar.

THE THALER OF MARIA THERESA

This coin was used during the time of the empress Maria Theresa, who ruled Bohemia and Hungary from 1740 to 1780. She was a kindhearted and greatly loved sovereign. During her reign, Vienna became the center of music and art. One of her many children was Marie Antoinette. The thaler, later spelled *taler,* was an important European coin for more than 400 years. From it comes our word dollar.

95

THE FRANC OF NAPOLEON

This coin was used during the life of Napoleon Bonaparte, who ruled France from 1799 to 1814. Under his command, French armies conquered all of Europe, including Austria, Prussia, Italy, Sweden, and Holland. Napoleon was finally defeated at Waterloo and exiled to the island of Saint Helena. The franc is still used in modern France. During Napoleon's time, the five-franc piece was made of silver. It carried a portrait of Napoleon wearing a wreath.

THE DOLLAR OF WASHINGTON AND LAFAYETTE

This coin was issued by the United States in 1900 to honor the Marquis de Lafayette, a French general who helped the American colonies win their independence. The obverse carries the profiles of Lafayette and George Washington. The reverse shows a statue of General Lafayette that was built in Paris. This monument was paid for by contributions from American school children. The Lafayette dollar is made of silver, and is the only commemorative dollar ever issued by this nation.

THE SHILLING OF NKRUMAH

This coin was used in Ghana, a nation located on the west coast of Africa. For over a hundred years this had been a British colony known as the Gold Coast. The country gained independence in 1957. In 1960 it became a republic within the British Commonwealth. Ghana symbolizes today's changing world, as many former colonies win nationhood. This coin, made of silver, was issued in amounts of 1, 2, and 10 shillings. It carries a portrait of Kwame Nkrumah, Ghana's first president.

A COIN OF THE FUTURE

This is a coin of tomorrow. It has not yet been issued, but the world will probably see it before very long. It will be struck to mark a great achievement. Perhaps it will honor the first man who set foot on the moon, or a world leader of peace, or the discoverer of an important new medicine. No one yet knows the issuing country. But the achievement will belong to *all* mankind, rather than to one country. This coin will mark a great step forward in the fascinating march of human history.

CLUBS, MUSEUMS, AND PUBLICATIONS

Part of the fun of an interesting hobby is sharing it with others. At present, there are more than two hundred and fifty coin clubs scattered throughout the United States. These are organized in almost every major city, and can be located through phone books, dealer shops, or coin publications. Joining a club enables us to meet other collectors to trade and sell items, take part in shows and auctions, and exchange gossip about the world of coins. There are also hundreds of coin-dealer shops located throughout the country, where catalogues and coins may be obtained, as well as the most current price information.

America has many splendid museums and exhibits of special interest to coin fanciers. Among these are the ones described on the following pages.

Roanoke Island,
North Carolina,
commemorative half dollar

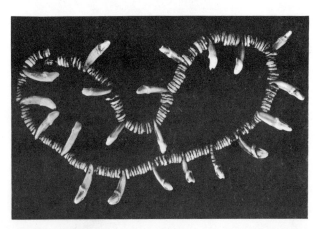

Canine teeth money from the Solomon Islands

Japanese bronze ten-yen piece

Bronze bell money
of Rhodesia

Japanese paper yen

The Smithsonian Institution, Washington, D.C.: This world-famed museum houses a display on the main floor, known as Numismatic Hall. It is a superb exhibit of coins, paper currency, and medals of both the United States and foreign lands. One section of this display shows the gradual evolution of money from primitive kinds, such as cowrie shells and wampum, to our present-day system of coinage and paper. Also on display are the official coin collection of the United States mint, dating back to the 1790's, and the largest collection of foreign gold coins shown anywhere in the world.

The American Numismatic Society, New York City: This building houses two great collections in facing halls. In one hall is a collection of world coins, containing many rare and unique specimens from the early days of Lydia to the present. These are arranged on special maps and charts, showing their exact place in man's history. The other hall has a beautiful display of medals and medallions from every part of the world. The Society also maintains one of the world's largest libraries of books and periodicals dealing with coins and currency.

Japanese gold oban

Roman as

U.S. postage currency

Stone money of Yap

*German coin
(denomination: 1 billion marks)*

Leather money of Mexico

"Ant's nose" money of China

U.S. colonial cent (privately minted)

Egyptian ring money (1000 B.C.)

The Chase Manhattan Bank Museum, New York City: This exhibit, known as the "Museum of Moneys of the World," is located in the center of Manhattan's theater and entertainment district. The display contains more than 75,000 specimens, starting with an ancient Babylonian "bill" written on clay more than 5,000 years ago. The Chase collection specializes in unique and unusual types of money. On display is a stone "coin" of Yap that measures 30 inches across and weighs 175 pounds.

Other outstanding American collections are in the Omaha Public Library, Omaha, Nebraska; the Museum of Fine Arts, Boston, Massachusetts; the exhibit at Boys Town, Nebraska; the Metropolitan Museum of Art, New York City; and the Buffalo Museum of Science, Buffalo, New York.

There are many magazines and periodicals of interest to coin collectors. Two fine newspapers are the "Numismatic News," published in Iola, Wisconsin; and "Coin World," published in Sidney, Ohio. Outstanding magazines are "The Numismatist," published by the American Numismatic Association in Wichita, Kansas; and "The Numismatic Scrapbook," issued by Hewitt Publications in Chicago, Illinois.

There are also many books dealing with different aspects of coins and collecting. Here is a suggested reading list for young collectors who wish to continue exploring this subject:

A Catalog of Modern World Coins . . . . R. S. Yeoman
Coin Dictionary and Guide . . . . C. C. Chamberlain and Fred Reinfeld
Coins and How to Know Them . . . . Gertrude B. Rawlings
Coins of Bible Days . . . . Florence Aiken Banks
Commemorative Coinage of the U.S. . . . . David M. Bullowa
The Complete Book of Coin Collecting . . . . Joseph Coffin
Confederate and Southern States Currency . . . . L. Bradbeer
Early Coins of America . . . . S. S. Crosby
Fell's International Coin Book . . . . Jacques Del Monte
Fell's United States Coin Book . . . . Jacques Del Monte
A Guide Book of United States Coins . . . . R. S. Yeoman
    (Contains average dealer's *selling* prices)
Handbook of United States Coins . . . . R. S. Yeoman
    (Contains average dealer's *buying* prices)
An Outline of Ancient Greek Coins . . . . Zander H. Klawans
Question and Answer Adventures with Coins . . . . . . Eva Knox Evans
Roman Coins and Medals . . . . Henry Cohen

A DICTIONARY FOR COIN COLLECTORS

ALLOY: A mixture of more than one metal.

BILINGUAL: Coinage or paper currency which carries words in two languages.

BULLION: Metal in bulk form, before being made into coins.

COMMEMORATIVE: A coin or medal issued in celebration of a person, place, or event.

CONDITION: The degree of wear, or lack of wear, visible on a particular coin.

CORRUGATED EDGE: An edge with vertical lines cut into it; also called a reeded edge.

Corrugated edge

COUNTERMARK: A special mark stamped over a coin design to show a new value, or a change in the issuing country.

DIE: A hard piece of metal containing a design from which coins are stamped.

DOUBLE EAGLE: United States $20 gold piece.

EAGLE: United States $10 gold piece.

ELECTRUM: A mixture of gold and silver.

Double Eagle

FACE VALUE: The original value marked on a coin. Example: 10 cents is the face value of a United States dime.

FASCES: A bundle of rods tied together, with an ax blade in the center; a symbol of authority in ancient Rome.

FIELD: The area behind the main figure on a coin; the background.

FLAN: A coin blank, the same as a planchet.

GUN MONEY: Coinage issued by King James II in 1689, made chiefly of metal from old cannons.

HALF EAGLE: United States $5 gold piece.

Fasces

INCUSE: A design sunk below the surface of a coin; just the opposite of the usual type of design, which is raised.

INSCRIPTION: Everything but the pictorial part of a coin; this includes all lettering, legends, and numerals.

LAUREATED: A coin portrait in which the head is crowned with a laurel wreath.

LEGEND: Wording on a coin which follows the curved line of the rim.

LETTERED EDGE: Lettering which appears around the vertical edge of a coin; used on some old United States half dollars and old European crowns.

MARKET VALUE: The price which a collector has to pay for a particular coin.

Laureated head

101

Module

Pattern coin

Obverse

Reverse

Token

MILLED EDGE: The coin rim, raised above the surface to form a tiny ledge.

MINT MARK: A small letter appearing on a coin to show the mint where the coin was made. On some European coins, the mint mark is a symbol rather than a letter.

MODULE: The diameter of a coin.

NUMISMATICS: The science and study of coins and medals.

OBVERSE: The front of a coin, or "heads."

OVERSTRIKE: A new impression, stamped on top of an earlier one, partly hiding the first.

PATINA: A greenish coating caused by oxidation, found on old copper coins.

PATTERN COINS: Experimental coins run off at a mint to test new designs or metals. These coins are not usually released to the public.

PLANCHET: The blank metal disc from which a coin is struck, also called a flan.

PREMIUM VALUE: The amount a coin is worth, over and above its face value.

PROOF: Coinage with a shiny, mirrorlike surface, minted especially for numismatists.

QUARTER EAGLE: United States $2.50 gold piece.

REEDED EDGE: An edge with up-and-down markings; also called a corrugated edge.

RESTRIKE: A coin made at a later date, but using the original dies.

REVERSE: The back of a coin, or "tails."

ROLL: A standard number, or stack, of identical coins, all of the same type, date, and mint.

TOKEN: A coinlike piece issued by individuals or companies, for advertising or other business purposes.

TYPE: A class of coins, based on the main design. Example: The United States Barber quarter is a type.

UNCIRCULATED: Coins which have never been put into general business use.

ABBREVIATIONS

AE: Copper
AR: Silver
AV: Gold
B: Brass
Br: Bronze
Bril.: Brilliant
C: Copper
CSSTP: Counterstamp
Diad.: Diademed

Ex. F.: Extremely Fine
F.: Fine
Fr.: Fair
G.: Good
Laur.: Laureated
Lg.: Large
Lib.: Liberty
MM: Mint mark
N: Nickel

Obv.: Obverse
R: Rare
RR: Very Rare
RRR: Extremely Rare
Rev.: Reverse
Sm.: Small
Unc.: Uncirculated
V.F.: Very Fine
V.G.: Very Good